The Emotions of Teacher Stress

Denise Carlyle and Peter Woods

Trentham Books

Stoke on Trent, UK and Sterling, USA

Trentham Books Limited

Westview House	22883 Quicksilver Drive
734 London Road	Sterling
Oakhill	VA 20166-2012
Stoke on Trent	USA
Staffordshire	
England ST4 5NP	

First published 2002

British Library Cataloguing-in-Publication Data
A catalogue record for this book is available from the British Library

1 85856 273 2

Designed and typeset by Trentham Print Design Ltd., Chester and printed in Great Britain by Cromwell Press Ltd., Wiltshire.

Contents

Acknowledgments

Many people have supported us in this research and helped directly and indirectly in the production of this book. Our special thanks go to all the teachers and their families who volunteered their stories. They willingly and openly explored emotional aspects of their personal and professional lives, sharing their vulnerability and emotional pain. During the first stages of the research, many were ill. Interviews were traumatic for some. It has been a joy and a privilege to participate in their recovery and self-renewal.

We are grateful to the National Union of Schoolmasters and Union of Women Teachers, to Steve Thorpe and Anne Hullis, and to Peter Pyranty of Stress at Work, for their help in finding our sample of teachers. They were also invaluable in providing insight into many aspects of teacher stress and counselling provision.

Our thanks go to Bob Jeffrey and Geoff Troman, members of our research team, for their informed contributions in our collaboration on teachers' work and stress, and their perceptive comments on our writing; to Piers Worth whose creativity and neurolinguistic skills aided theorising and progressive focusing; to Lesley Roberts for peer supervision, enthusiasm and generous friendship. We are grateful to Gillian Klein for her support and encouragement throughout the writing of the book, and for many valuable and helpful suggestions on the original manuscript. The book would have been the poorer but for these contributions, though we must accept responsibility for the final text and any imperfections that remain. Our thanks also go to Aileen Cousins and Alison Leslie for their valuable secretarial support and to Jan Giddings for her thorough transcription of interview tapes that held sensitive and distressing information.

This research was funded by The Open University. The faith, encouragement and support given by the Centre for Sociology and Social Research at the School of Education, and by Alison Robinson is warmly acknowledged.

Earlier versions of chapters were presented as papers at: the British Educational Research Association Conferences at the University of Belfast, (1988) (chapter 2) and the University of Sussex, (1999) (chapter 5); and at the Ethnography and Education Conference at Oxford (1998) (methodology). We are appreciative of the comments of participants at these conferences in the critiquing and development of ideas.

Finally, special thanks go to Dr Julia Boon for believing in post-polio syndrome, and for her advice, understanding and support; to Diane and Carole for the gifts of time and attention; and to Chris, Ewan and Annie whose 'warm fuzzies', love, humour, encouragement and practical support made this possible.

Abbreviations

ATL: Association of Teachers and Lecturers

BERA: British Educational Research Association

DfEE: Department for Education and Employment

DoH: Department of Health

EBD: Emotional and Behavioural Difficulties

ESAC: Education Service Advisory Committee

GNVQ: General National Vocational Qualifications

GP: General Practitioner

HASAWA: Health and Safety at Work Act

HoD: Head of Department

HSE: Health and Safety Executive

MHSW: Management of Health and Safety at Work

NACCCE: National Advisory Committee on Creative and Cultural Education

NAHT: National Association of Head Teachers

NASUWT: National Association of Schoolmasters and Women Teachers

NUT: National Union of Teachers

NQT: Newly Qualified Teacher

NWN: National Work-stress Network

Ofsted: Office for Standards in Education

SEN: Special Educational Needs

SMT: Senior Management Team

TBF: Teachers' Benevolent Fund

TUC: Trade Union Council

Introduction: Teacher Stress and The Emotions

In an age of rapid escalation in the rates of general occupational stress (Cooper, 2000), teaching is one of the most stressful occupations (Travers and Cooper, 1996; Kyriacou, 2000). An increasing stream of letters and articles in the educational press gives voice to both teacher and teacher families' accounts of teacher stress. Teacher retirements on the grounds of ill-health in England and Wales rose from 2698 in 1985/86 to 6075 in 1994/95 (Robinson, 1997). In 1996, 13,000 teachers left teaching early, an increase of 50 per cent on 1986 (Rafferty, 1997). In 1997, 37.4 per cent of vacancies in secondary schools were reported as due to ill-health retirement (Salmon, 1997). By 1997, early retirement was estimated as annually costing £480 million (Robinson, 1997).

In response, the Government altered pension rules in 1997, making it more difficult for teachers to retire early, adding to the decline in morale and prompting fears of an 'ageing, sick profession' (Rafferty, 1997). Premature and ill-health retirements showed a significant drop, but already are creeping back up again (in England, 4,740 in 1998-9, 5,800 in 2000-1) (DfES, 2002a). Teacher unions report 'a torrent of stress claims pending' (Comerford and Mansell, 1999), the National Association of Schoolmasters and Women Teachers (NASUWT) handling 120 cases in the year 2000, the National Union of Teachers (NUT) 180 cases, the Association of Teachers and Lecturers (ATL) 40 cases, and the National Association of Head Teachers (NAHT) 25 cases (Henry, 2000). A rising number of teachers have secured compensation for stress-related illness (Bunting, 1999). Teacher stress has thus become 'a serious problem for the local authorities, governing bodies and the Government itself to tackle' (Graham Clayton, senior NUT solicitor, in Comerford and Mansell, 1999).

There is increasing concern regarding the far-reaching costs and consequences for education and the situation still appears to be worsening. DfEE statistics (2002a) report 55 per cent of all teachers in England taking sickness absence in 1999, and 56% in 2000. 2,503,300 days in 1999 and 2,664,400 days in 2000 are estimated to have been lost through illness. In 2000, 45 per cent of absences were for at least twenty working days, showing extended illness. The cost of all absences is in the region of £3 million. In addition, there is a crisis of recruitment and retention within the profession, growing numbers of teachers having retired early with stress-related ill-health (Smithers and Robinson, 1998), and a large proportion of new teachers leaving either during training or within five years of taking up their first post. At 31 March, 2001, an estimated 296,000 qualified teachers aged under 60 in England alone were out of service. A further 83,000 have never been in service. Travers and Cooper (1996) found two-thirds of their large national sample had actively considered leaving teaching within the previous five years.

A growing body of research connects rises in teacher stress to the restructuring of educational systems, which has been going on contemporaneously (Farber, 1991; Hargreaves, 1994; Woods *et al*, 1997; Dinham and Scott, 1996; Fullan, 1997; Brown and Ralph, 1998). Major societal change and radical, swift changes in governmental policies have created new demands of educational institutions and teaching staff (Hargreaves, 1994). A raft of legislation, beginning with the 1988 Education Reform Act, mandating Local Management of Schools, inspections, assessments and testing, and league tables, with, following the Act, multiple amendments to the National Curriculum every few years, has propelled schools through a period of continuous, governmentally imposed change (Brown and Ralph, 1998). Teachers' work has intensified (Apple, 1986; Hargreaves, 1994). Research by the Teachers' Benevolent Fund (2000) suggests that 93,000 teachers experience severe workplace stress resulting from excessive workloads. There are reports of increasing conflict with managers and colleagues, indicating problems with the health of both school and teaching environments (*ibid*). Professional models of the 'good teacher' and 'good teaching' have become areas of contestation (Troman, 1996; Kelchtermans, 1996). Brown and Ralph (1998) suggest a turbulent environment ripe for stress and burnout was created by change overload, the ways changes were introduced and managed, the speed of implementation allowing little time for reflection, and the weight of responsibility on teachers.

Much time and effort has been spent researching teacher stress, with little apparent benefit. Despite being a well documented matter of international concern (Byrne, 1995) – in Britain (Kyriacou, 1987; HSE, 1990; Woods, 1995); Germany, Scandinavia and Russia (Rudow, 1995); the United States of America (Farber, 1991); Israel (Friedman, 1991); Canada (Leithwood *et al*, 1995); Australia (Dinham, 1993); and Hong Kong (Chan and Hui, 1995) stress and stress-related illness continue to escalate (Troman and Woods, 2001), with 'serious implications for work performance, health and psychological status' (Pithers, 1995: 387). While stress is acknowledged as a 'multi-dimensional and multi-levelled phenomenon', involving micro (personal), meso (organisational) and macro (structural) factors (Woods, 1996a: 1), much research on stress has treated these three elements as discrete entities (Kelchtermans, 1995) rather than as inter-related phenomena. Much stress research, by espousing the 'orthodox categorisation of the person as a psychological entity distinct from the social milieu, though influenced by it' (Handy, 1990: 5), fostered a false separation of the individual and the social context. This encouraged the adoption of a discourse of individual responsibility, where people are deemed vulnerable to stress due to unique personal profiles (Newton *et al*, 1995). Handy (1995) argues that many psychological models, purportedly adopting a more interactional stance encompassing meso and micro perspectives, nonetheless continue to have an individual basis. In placing the individual at the centre, they emphasise the differences between people at the expense of their commonalities. While Handy agrees that stress is 'undeniably a subjective psychological experience' (*ibid*: 87), she shows how one effect of such discourses is the depoliticisation of work stress, since such accounts fail to recognise how shared perceptions and actions, produced through shared working experiences, may lead to organisational adaptational processes (Stapley, 1996).

A focus solely on teacher-centred causes and solutions fails to address collective influences on individual and organisational health and performance, the inter-relationships between micro-meso-macro factors, or the reasons why individuals and groups adopt particular coping strategies and behaviours (Cox *et al*, 1989). While personal coping strategies may be effective in mitigating some pressures, individuals may have little control over sources of, and solutions to, stress at institutional levels (Crawford, 1997). Blase (1991) argues that political aspects of school environments are crucial to understanding stress. He agrees with Ball (1987) and Sparkes (1990), that much political activity in schools is accompanied by significant stress, and that teachers increasingly associate strong, intensely negative feelings with school-based micro-politics. While there have been a number of studies of school micro-politics (for example, Ball, 1987), there have been fewer of the strong emotions involved, their nature, causes and effects. Since the latter are profound, with severe repercussions for individuals and institutions, they are worthy of more focused study.

Emotion and Teacher Stress

We follow the European Commission's (2000) definition of work stress as

> the emotional, cognitive, behavioural and physiological reaction to aversive and noxious aspects of work, work environments and work organisations. It is a state characterised by high levels of arousal and distress and often by feelings of not coping.

In viewing stress as an outcome of both social and psychological forces, it becomes clear that there are both positive and negative aspects to stress. Stress in moderation is an important motivational factor. Positive stress, or 'Eustress' (Selye, 1974), characterised by 'a healthy sense of being stretched and challenged and sufficiently well-supported to meet the challenge', is energising and enhances performance (Veninga and Spradley, 1981: 37). For us, this is more like healthy professional pressure. We are concerned with stress in its negative aspects.

We follow Veninga and Spradley's (1981: 6-7) view of burnout as primarily caused by

> unrelieved stress, the kind that goes on day after day, month after month, year after year .... a debilitating psychological condition ....

> which results in depleted energy resources, lowered resistance to illness, increased dissatisfaction and pessimism, increased absenteeism and inefficiency at work.

We view individual burnout as primarily a social and cultural phenomenon (Bartlett, 1998; Sarason, 1996). As Freudenberger, who first brought the term to public consciousness, proposed, society can be seen as the 'breeder' of burnout through 'eroding tradition, banishing our support systems, barricading minority groups, and dissolving relationships' (Freudenberger and Richelson, 1980: 198), creating an environment where 'energy has turned to ennui, the enthusiasm into anger, the optimism to despair' (*ibid*: xiv). The experience of stress generates much distressing emotion, such as anxiety, guilt, shame, and sadness (Eisler and Blalock, 1991). Stress and emotion are thus 'intimately connected' (Lazarus and Lazarus, 1994: 238).

Emotions are complex cognitive structures linking feeling, thinking and action (Ekman and Davidson, 1994; Averill, 1996), giving 'shape and meaning to somatic and affective experiences' (Shweder, 1994: 37). According to Crawford *et al* (1992: 37), they are

> produced in people's attempts to make sense of their world, in their efforts to appropriate and resist the structures of their everyday lives: they are the stuff out of which people construct and evaluate selves.

Emotions 'lie at the heart of teaching' (Hargreaves, 1998a: 835), emotional bonds filling teachers' relationships with students, parents and colleagues, binding teaching strategies and conceptual thinking (Jeffrey and Woods, 1996). Teachers have a deep emotional relationship to their work, due not only to this relational orientation but also to the high investment of the self in their work and the heavy investment in time, goals, moral purposes, commitments and attachments that they make within their working lives (Nias, 1996). Teaching is thus an 'emotional practice' (Hargreaves, 1998a), 'highly charged with feeling, aroused by and directed towards not just people but also values and ideals' (Nias, 1996: 293). Hargreaves (1998a: 835) contends that 'good teachers' are 'emotional, passionate beings who connect with their students and fill their work and their classes with pleasure, creativity, challenge and joy', and where 'good teaching' is 'charged with positive emotion'. Many teachers speak of feeling 'love' for their students (Nias, 1989; Hargreaves, 1998a). However, there are reports that negative emotion is increasingly evident in teachers' working lives, a survey of teachers' attitudes revealing 'a tired, angry profession with an agenda for change' (Sutcliffe, 1997). Jeffrey and Woods' (1996) teachers reported feeling 'fear, anguish, anger, despair, depression, humiliation, grief and guilt'. Hargreaves and Tucker (1991) observe that guilt, in particular, with associated feelings of frustration and anxiety, is a central preoccupation of teachers, which demotivates and disables. They argue that guilt is not a personal choice but a public issue, socially generated and mediated, emotionally located and practically consequential.

One of the main changes noticed in recent years has been a shift in teachers' emotionality, the process of 'being emotional', which 'locates the person in the world of social interaction' (Denzin, 1984: 137). Nias (1996: 300) reports that while students were formerly reported as occupying the central emotional role, currently, the 'most intensive, hostile and deeply disturbing emotions' come from encounters with other adults, and from 'intrusions on professional territory' from school policy such as maintaining records and disciplinary interventions. Halton (1995: 187-189) suggests that structural changes within current educational institutions have been disabling, resulting in 'cultures of conflict' and 'atmospheres of hostility and mistrust', with 'lives turned upside down', and staff filled with 'anger, fear and despair'. Supporting Fineman (1993), regarding the lack of attention paid to negative emotion within organisational research, Hargreaves (1999) highlights how much literature on teacher feeling and emotion focuses on the more easily managed and apparently safer emotions, such as satisfaction and dissatisfaction (Dinham and Scott, 1996), rather than on the more unsettling, volatile, unpredictable emotions such as joy, excitement, frustration, anxiety, sadness, jealousy, envy, fear, guilt, shame and anger, which often signal the presence of stress (Lazarus and Lazarus, 1994; Oatley, 1996).

While teacher emotion is experienced individually, it arises through ongoing transactions within social relationships (Parkinson, 1996). An emphasis on rationality, predominantly derived from psychological perspectives, led to an individualised discourse on teacher emotion, a discourse of positive emotion, and a lack of understanding of how the emotional landscapes of teaching are formed through social transactions, shaped not only by individuals, but also by sociological, political and institutional forces (Blackmore, 1996). In particular, until recently, there has been little sociological analysis into the emotions of teaching. Richardson (1995: 67), in exploring how educational change processes deeply affect emotional relationships constituting the heart of teaching and learning, emphasises the relational aspect of stress, constantly feeling undervalued, feeling responsible for the ills of society, feeling contempt and disrespect from students, feeling the government's lack of faith in the profession, feeling media scorn, where 'stress is caused by feeling bad about oneself and constantly being made aware of one's inadequacy even though one is actually quite good at the job'. As Nias (1996: 305) contends, emotion therefore is not simply '*in* teaching', but is a response to working conditions, and the increasing need to defend the self. Hargreaves (1998b: 315) agrees, seeing the emotional lives of teachers not just as 'matters of personal disposition or commitment, as psychological qualities that emerge among individuals' but as 'social and political phenomena ... shaped by how the work of teaching is organized, structured and led'.

Although the links between stress and emotion are well documented, a consideration of these associations is missing from many conceptual accounts of stress (Lazarus and Lazarus, 1994). Many models of teacher stress have been criticised for not paying enough attention to affective components (Boyle *et al*, 1995). Hargreaves (1998a) claims that many involved in educational reform, and in writing about educational change, underplay the emotional dimension. Psychological and sociological research into stress and emotion within industrial and business contexts demonstrates the importance of considering organisations as emotional arenas (Litwin *et al*, 1978; Fassel, 1992; Newton *et al*, 1995; Stapley, 1996). While much is known about which emotions teachers feel, little is known of the relational and organisational processes surrounding these emotions. As Hargreaves and Fullan (1998) point out, understanding change processes requires deeper analysis, plus the commitment to translate ideas and understandings into action, where greater attention needs to be paid in particular to the emotions of educational change. Kyriacou (1987: 146) defines teacher stress as 'the experience by a teacher of unpleasant emotions, such as tension, frustration, anxiety, anger and depression, resulting from aspects of his work as a teacher', and burnout as the result of 'prolonged teacher stress, primarily characterised by physical, emotional and attitudinal exhaustion'. Despite this emphasis on emotional components, much research on teacher stress and burnout tells us very little about how teachers experience stress and burnout socially, politically and phenomenologically, how micro-political factors impinge on the stress process, and how stress emotions are linked to illness careers.

Williams (1998: 124) argues that emotions 'underpin the phenomenological experience of our bodies in sickness and health', providing the 'basis for social reciprocity and exchange and the 'link' between personal problems and broader public issues of social structure'. Emotion is vital in understanding the relationship between stress and illness. As Brown and Harris (1989: 133) state,

> the fact that socio-economic factors now primarily affect health through psychosocial rather than material pathways, places emotions centre-stage in the social patterning of disease and disorder in advanced Western societies.

Emotion thus lies 'at the heart of the aetiological process' (Williams, 1998: 126), playing a 'central role in the human experience and cultural scripts of health, sickness, disability and death' (Williams and Bendelow, 1996: 47). Illness narratives provide insight into emotion as the missing sociological link between the micro effect of macro issues and the macro effect of micro issues (Freund, 1990; Hyden 1997).

In this book, therefore, we focus on achieving a better understanding of the emotional processes influencing stress within secondary schools, and the relationships between stress, individual and organisational emotion, and individual and organisational health. We adopt a 'communicative approach' to emotion where emotion is viewed as social, as part of 'a process of making claims about personal or social identity to particular intended audiences in the context of unfolding social encounters' (Parkinson, 1995: 169). As Wilkinson (1996: 184) points out, stress emotions, such as 'a sense of desperation, anger, bitterness, learned helplessness or aggression', are 'all wholly understandable responses to various social, economic and material difficulties'. Seeking out some of the major research omissions, we argue that, due to an emphasis on teacher-based causes and solutions, the underlying structural factors of stress are poorly understood and inadequately dealt with, and that a consideration of social processes surrounding individual and collective emotion is fundamental to understanding teacher stress.

Research Methods

The emotional lives of twenty-one secondary teachers were explored through qualitative accounts using open-ended, semi-structured, in-depth life history interviews. Eleven men and ten women, aged between twenty-five and fifty-eight, were interviewed between two and nine times over a period of twelve months between 1996 and 1998. Some characteristics of this group are shown in table 1. As we were seeking close, intimate detail of experiences that had been extremely painful to them, we took great care in the selection of the sample. They had to meet the following criteria: a) our operational definition of stress, which was that they had experienced stress-related illness that had been professionally diagnosed by a GP, counsellor, or psychiatrist, and had incurred significant absence from school within the past five years; b) they had to be able and willing to talk to us, in full knowledge of the aims and methods of the research; and c) in the opinions of all concerned, they were unlikely to suffer any ill-effects as a result of participating (see below for how this was handled in the research). They came from four sources:

1. The research began with four teachers whom Denise had previously met while teaching in a sixth form consortium. Contact with these teachers was initially made at the suggestion of a friend in Castlerigg Comprehensive. Two of these teachers (one male, one female) had left teaching, taking voluntary early retirement. Two (one male, one female) had returned to teaching after a period of stress-related illness. One of these interviews led to contact with a fifth participant, Gareth, from this same school, who was now in other employment.
2. Later, we consulted a local authority service offering stress management courses to schools and counselling to teachers. They sent letters to eighteen schools on their Stress Facilitators

Table 1. Characteristics of the sample of teachers

Teacher	Family members	Age	Position prior to stress illness	School location
Alex	Angie	37	Science, second in department	Walton Green, urban comprehensive
Andrew	Sarah	44	Science teacher	Walton Green, urban comprehensive
Jonathon	Jo	44	Head of Business, GNVQ co-ordinator	Walton Green, urban comprehensive
Margot	Stuart	42	Arts teacher	Walton Green, urban comprehensive
Charlotte	Daniel	47	Drama teacher	Castlerigg, town comprehensive
Edward	Olivia	51	Science teacher	Castlerigg, town comprehensive
Gareth	Marjorie	57	Science teacher, part-time	Castlerigg, town comprehensive
Maureen	Graham	51	Arts teacher	Castlerigg, town comprehensive
Ralph	Gina, Fiona, Paul	46	Humanities teacher, Head of Year	Castlerigg, town comprehensive
Morag	N/A	25	Arts teacher	Gaines Park, urban comprehensive
Rachel	Matthew, Hannah, Michael	46	French teacher, GNVQ Health and Care	Gaines Park, urban comprehensive
Celia	Hector,	36	Music, sole in department	rural comprehensive
Emily	Robert	53	Science teacher	urban comprehensive
Jessica	Frank	45	Home economics teacher	town comprehensive
Luke	Shirley	37	Maths, second in department	urban comprehensive
Marcus	Pauline	50	French teacher	town comprehensive
Rebecca	N/A	45	Head of English	urban middle school
Sally	Ivor	38	English teacher	urban comprehensive
Stephen	Jenny	50	Mathematics, GNVQ core, IT co-ordinator	town comprehensive
Terence	Alicia	50	Deputy Head, Geography teacher	urban comprehensive
William	Lindsey	51	Head of Science	urban middle school

Note: School is not named in cases where teachers were the sole member of staff to be interviewed.

Network list. Yvonne, a deputy head in Walton Green, the only school to reply, contacted us with the names of four teachers who agreed to interviews. An interview with Yvonne later gave some insight into organisational responses to stress-related illness within Walton Green. A subsequent interview with her had to be cancelled as she herself was absent due to stress-related illness, and shortly took early retirement because of ill-health.

3. The charity Stress at Work offers independent counselling services, seminars and courses. We met with counsellor/manager Peter Pyranty, who sent letters to some teacher clients he judged sufficiently recovered from stress-related illness to safely take part in this research. Four volunteered to tell their story, a fifth teacher later becoming part of the sample. Denise later interviewed Peter Pyranty to ascertain his ideas about the nature and course of teacher stress.

4. Finally, three participants were obtained through direct teacher union contacts, and four answered advertisements placed in union magazines.

So this is not a representative sample – that would have been even more difficult to assemble, given the criteria. But this was not necessary for our purposes, which was to acquire a new depth of understanding and insights into the emotions experienced by teachers undergoing stress-related illness and the connection between those emotions and the social and structural conditions in which the teachers worked and lived. We would claim that the results of the research have relevance for all teachers since their reaction to experiences that all teachers face to some degree, rather than experiences unique to themselves, renders the teachers in our sample 'critical cases' (Hammersley and Atkinson, 1995). As such, they highlight the issues concerned in sharp detail.

One further point needs to be made about the sample. It might be thought that these teachers were in some way personally emotionally 'vulnerable', or professionally 'incompetent'. However, apart from newly qualified teacher (NQT) Morag, all had had lengthy careers with many happy years in teaching and records of successful appraisals, inspections and examination results. Indeed Margot was one of the first teachers to be given an Award of Excellence.

The majority of our teachers taught in schools where attainment on entry was below national standard, or, in the cases of Sally and Celia, severely below. Rebecca, Sally and Celia's schools were under 'special measures'. 'Serious weaknesses' in Rebecca's middle school of around 280 pupils included 'low standards of attainment in English and mathematics; inadequate standards of pupils' behaviour; unsatisfactory teaching in about a quarter of lessons; weak curriculum planning and assessment; and unresolved long-term staffing difficulties' (www.ofsted.gov.uk). Celia's 11-18 rural comprehensive of around 600 pupils had 15.4% on free school meals (around the national average) and 27.9% with special needs (above the national average), of which sixteen (3.8%) were statemented (above the national average). In Sally's urban comprehensive of 831 students, poor attendance records and difficulties recruiting and retaining staff, 50% of students had special needs and eighteen were statemented. Here 37% had free school meals, and English was an additional language for 9%. Exclusions were higher than the national average, numbering 69 fixed period and five permanent. In contrast, 21.1% of the 1000 students in Marcus' school had special educational needs and 1.8% had statements (both around the national average), and in William's school it was 13.5% and four students with statements, and few children in either had free school meals.

Ten interviewees taught in two schools, so allowing for some corroboration of accounts. Gareth, Charlotte, Maureen, Edward and Ralph taught in Castlerigg, an 11-18 town comprehensive with just over 750 students of below national average student attainment on entry. Of these students 34% had special educational needs, ten with special provision and eight with statements, and 16.7% had free school meals. The 1996 Ofsted report notes staffing problems due to long-term absence and difficulties in providing specialist cover, and 20 fixed period and seven permanent exclusions.

Andrew, Margot, Jonathon and Alex taught in Walton Green, a large 13-18 urban comprehensive with over 1270 pupils, with 'a significant minority of students suffering some socio-economic deprivation' that provided 'a sound education supported by good teaching in a caring environment' (*ibid*). Here 32.3% of students had special educational needs and 18.8% free school meals. The 1996 Ofsted inspection reports numbers of exclusions as 31 fixed period and seven permanent. Key issues for action include the need for 'urgent' addressing of monitoring and appraisal structures and processes, and the consistent application of whole school policies (*ibid*).

In Rachel and Morag's urban 13-18 comprehensive of just under 450 students, 30% of students had free school meals, exclusions numbered 29 fixed period and three permanent, 6% held a statement of special needs, and for 15%, English was an additional language. Jessica's town comprehensive was the largest, with 1430 on the roll, 25% of whom had special needs, 28 of them statemented. Ethnic minority students made up 12.8% and 8.6% of students had free school meals. Exclusions numbered 57 fixed period and six permanent.

The longitudinal nature of the interviews allowed us to gain an overall view of the progress of illness. Participants were at different stages in the illness trajectory (Strauss, 1987), some receiving therapeutic interventions such as counselling and medication during or after long-term absence, some well into the recovery process, others experiencing false recoveries and relapse. All participants were fragile and vulnerable. The exploration of sensitive issues encourages people to share their emotional distress and disclose confidential and personal information (Brannen, 1988). According to Lee (1993: 4), such sensitive research 'potentially poses a substantial threat to those who are or have been involved in it' and may present problems, 'because research into them involves potential costs to those involved in the research, including, on occasion, the researcher'. The nature of the research task thus required planning to carry out ethically responsible research (Sieber, 1992), minimizing research risks to interviewees and interviewer while pursuing the goal of uncovering sensitive information through exploring emotionally charged arenas. Accordingly, Denise adopted a humanistic framework for interviewing derived from person-centred counselling (Mearns and Thorne, 1988; Paterson, 1997). This both encouraged a facilitative relationship and provided protection by minimising risks. For a full account of this aspect of the research, see Carlyle (2000).

Nine spouses agreed to interview, initially for triangulation and validation purposes, and to investigate the illness trajectory. In two families, teenage children also volunteered their experiences. Interviews took place mainly in teachers' homes, save for six in the workplace, and generally lasted two to three hours, of which about one and a half hours was taped. Teachers and their families discussed their biographies, the factors affecting the onset of illness, the experience of illness, factors inhibiting and facilitating self-renewal, interactions with connecting spheres such as the family and the employment of spouses. All participants were encouraged to tell their stories in their own way (Atkinson, 1998; Rubin and Rubin, 1995). Interviews were recorded on tape and professionally transcribed, analytical summaries returned for validation and additional comment. Analysis was through comparative analysis, the identification of major themes and categories, and 'grounded theory' (Strauss and Corbin, 1990).

All the names of the teachers, families and schools are fictitious.

Overview of Chapters

The first two chapters are concerned with teachers' perceptions of the major factors originating their stress. The main sites were school and home, and stress was often a product of interaction between the two. While bearing this in mind, we treat the sites separately. Chapter 1 considers the teachers' experiences at their schools which they saw as contributing to the onset of stress. We link changes in teachers' emotionality with micropolitical processes within modified school cultures. The schools had negative emotional structures and showed poor leadership, divisive hierarchies, poor lines of communication, autocratic decision-making and bullying management styles. The result was negative emotional climates derived from the government's emphasis on managerialism, rational-technicism, performativity and heavy accountability. The schools were not happy places and they were characterised by fear, worry, distrust, blame and low respect. Low levels of emotional literacy and awareness were found among management and among staff generally. Emotional expression was not encouraged in these institutions, a considerable problem given the sharp increase in emotional labour our teachers experienced. An accepted and important component of teachers' professional activity and skill, emotional labour with colleagues and with pupils, had become burdensome emotional toil. Finally, we note the phenomenon of the 'stress cascade' – how stress is passed on from one sphere to another, from government to school management to staff to pupils, and back again – and perhaps on to families. In this sense, once started, stress is a self-generative and self-sustaining system.

Chapter two considers stress within the home. For these teachers and their families, the home offered no refuge from tensions in the workplace. Stress cascaded across interconnecting spheres. Emotional transactions in family life often compounded problems within the working sphere and vice versa. We look at key life events influencing stress levels in the family – coping with quadruple shifts, bereavement and illness, children's problems, possibly marital difficulties, and the impact of the teachers' stress and burnout on family relationships and family health. There is spillover of stress between home and work, one aggravating the other, the stress worsening in the interplay. In the circumstances of the families of our teachers, the transactions between the home and work tip each other over the edge in a spiral of decline. Emotional climates and competences deteriorate, emotional labour increases and becomes unmanageable, leading to deterioration in health, in relationships and in identities.

We argue that during stress teachers undergo a passage of identity. This process begins with separation from the personal identities teachers have constructed over the years, passes through a transitional phase before re-engagement and identity reconstruction gets under way. Chapters three to five are concerned with these three phases. Chapter three charts how, during the onset of stress, many cherished aspects of the self are attacked and become separated from the teachers' personal identity. Before their stress, teachers enjoyed esteemed and stable identities, with consistency between the demands of the teacher role and their own values, and between work and home. Teaching was a personally rewarding job. During the first phase of stress, teachers lose the intrinsic rewards of teaching, lose control and autonomy, collegiality, emotional skills, awareness and regulation, and become emotionally estranged. The experience of stress negatively affected learning situations. Teachers became less successful at managing stressful social transactions with colleagues and students. This increased the levels of stress for teachers and their students, many of whom were already highly stressed by their home lives. Professional competence was compromised through emotive dissonance, which fed feelings of failure. Stressed teachers became 'failing' teachers. As negative emotion accumulated, ontological security was threatened and its loss caused emotional breakdown. The teachers have little time or space to attend to these problems, the intensification of workloads leaving no space for reflexivity. Physical as well as emotional health becomes affected as teachers lose all sense of who they are. A relentless spiral pulls them down to the depths of despair.

In chapter four, we examine the transitional phase, in which teachers experience the catastrophic terror of 'hitting rock bottom' but also begin to detect glimmers of hope of 're-birthing'. They responded to a 'cocooning' process, whereby they found space for the necessary process of grieving over lost selves (Nias, 1989), beginning identity work and recovery of the self, and reaching new emotional understanding. Significant others – family members, doctors, counsellors – helped in the social cushioning and re-empowering of the self, raising awareness, providing social contextualising for their stress, assuaging the teachers' sense of guilt and blame. Gradually the teachers recovered their physical and emotional health, rediscovered their creativity and sense of control, and began to re-engage with the world. They modified roles to assist them in this task. But recovery was not straightforward. There was no smooth, continuous passage back to an ideal normality. As re-engagement brought teachers back to the real world, they inevitably faced dilemmas presented by that world and the part they were to play in it. Sometimes, decisions they made or events set them back a step or two after they had made some progress.

For some, at least, there was fuller 'self-renewal'. Reflection led them to re-assess their working environments. Some sought to change those environments to suit their own self-concept better, or sought a compromise between role and self. Others changed their environments completely, moving to other schools or out of teaching altogether. A few were finding it difficult to achieve the transition to self-renewal. A basic factor for success was finding positive emotional experiences and re-establishing consistency between the demands of the job and their own self-concept. The teachers' testimony mirrors the downward spiral related in chapter three, together with repairs to the negativities reported in chapter one. In these new situations, we see the emergence of trust, control, autonomy, collegiality, respect, de-intensification, democratic management, good communication, positive emotional climates. Some of our teachers reinvented and re-empowered themselves through spiritual fulfilment, and/or finding new knowledge and understanding, and/or actively seeking to heighten their levels of emotional literacy. Thus, while a few were still stuck within 'spoiled identities', some at the other end of the scale were claiming to have grown stronger and better as a result of the stress experience.

In chapter six we examine the implications of our research for policy-making at national, school and individual levels, bearing in mind the interdependence of system, organisational and individual affect, and of personal and collective emotional competences and emotional climates. Interestingly, we are beginning to hear in official statements some recognition of how government policy needs to change – the most important item – though it remains to be seen how much remains mere rhetoric. Whatever changes are made, schools do not have to take up a position within the 'stress cascade' but can instead act as an interrupting force. They do not have to be run on hierarchical, bullying, instrumental, negative emotional lines. We discuss how schools can prevent stress by putting appropriate systems in place and developing a supportive and healthy work environment and positive emotional climates. Also, managers in school need to be able to detect signs of stress early and to head it off before the downward spiral and spillover begins to take hold. And if some have gone down that route despite all precautions, then they need to receive appropriate rehabilitation and recovery processes.

Finally, we consider what individuals can do to ward off or cope with stress. Agency can be strengthened. Knowledge is power. Political understanding of the social circumstances that shape and possibly constrain their personal identities combined with a high level of emotional awareness and competences applied to both themselves and others, is a potent recipe for recovery.

1

Origins of Stress 1: 'Eggshell Days' in School

There is no single cause of stress. Rather than trying to identify causes, or the main causes, we find it more meaningful to explore how stress arose in the first place and how it developed. What were the circumstances that led to stress? What social structures, aspects of life, features of one's roles and interactions with others came into question? What norm-disrupting incidents occurred, provoking what reactions? How does stress take root, develop and escalate?

For our teachers, the main sites of stress were school and family and the interaction between the two was especially aggravating, as stress spilled over and exacerbated feelings in the other sphere. In chapters 1 and 2 we consider the origins of stress as seen by our teachers, first in the school, then in the family. The effect of 'spillover' will become clear in chapter 2.

As far as school is concerned, much of the problem was seen to reside in negative emotional structures, inadequate and ill-designed to cope with the vast changes of the late 1980s and 1990s. These structures bred negative emotional climates, low levels of emotional literacy, and high levels of emotional labour. We consider each of these in turn.

Negative Emotional Structures

Negative emotions were seen to stem from crisis management, poor communication systems, autocratic decision-making, and bullying management styles.

Crisis management

Teachers perceived schools as ill-equipped to manage change. Alex spoke of 'so much crisis management. People setting up poor systems'. They reported poor leadership and insensitive professional challenge, 'divisive hierarchies' with 'conflict amongst individual senior staff ... We're not good at feeding back, not good at identifying people's strengths and skills' (Yvonne, deputy head in Walton Green). Teachers received no training in change management. Those responsible for managing change found colleagues highly resistant to further change without rewards. Alex, for example, employed 'to bring in new approaches' to Walton Green, had 'a vision' of 'more active learning ... to alter thought processes, then techniques'. However, teachers were 'frightened of change'. Delegation proved difficult. 'They're locked into the idea: You get paid for it. You do the work'.

Much teacher stress was perceived as originating in school mergers:

> The stress goes all the way back to the creation of the school (Ralph).

> Everybody was up for grabs, didn't know if they were going to keep their job. Everybody was stressed. It wasn't just me, the whole school. (Maureen)

School mergers have been one of the most radical externally imposed innovations schools have faced in the wake of educational reform. Re-organisation has incurred huge costs in teacher and student stress, and in school effectiveness (Draper, 1992; Kyriacou and Harriman, 1993; McHugh and Kyle, 1993). The merging of Woodend Boys School and Garthfell Girls School to form Castlerigg Comprehensive created such problems. Groups of teachers polarised by their differing educational philosophies, some of them demoted, resisted change. Edward, for example, who along with five of his faculty colleagues previously enjoyed Head of Department (HoD) status, described his department as feeling 'under attack, identified as not succeeding, and vulnerable' because of 'poor results and some poor teaching' in the post-merger culture. They 'failed to accept the new regime' and their opposition fed back into the destabilisation of the school. He noted the lack of skills in collective and individual change management:

> The school should have realised the amalgamation was going to be stressful. Among the four Deputy Heads somebody could have been given responsibility to oversee and identify things causing trouble. (Edward)

Gareth, who joined the department in the third year after amalgamation, corroborated Edward's account, reporting 'severe historical problems', 'low morale', 'a lousy department' with 'poor materials, poor motivation, poor teaching and poor discipline. It was dog eat dog, a recipe for disaster'.

The situation during the change process at Castlerigg was exacerbated by 'conflict between schools of teaching' (Ralph). There was no open discussion or professional development available for those who had no experience of co-educational teaching and found it difficult. Maureen 'tried really hard with the boys' but 'the discipline aspect just got harder and harder'. Ralph reported struggling with a new line manager from the girls' school, 'a middle-aged spinster, never had any children, hadn't the faintest idea how to handle teenage boys'. According to Draper (1992: 371), school mergers can cause some male teachers and boys to try to establish 'traditional gender codes of dominance' over other staff and students. At Castlerigg teachers from the girls' school saw their teaching styles disappear as the teaching style used in the boys' school became dominant:

> We had to bark at students, shout at them, be aggressive in our attitudes, raise your voice, yell down the corridors. I couldn't do that. It was completely alien to me. That was at the core of my really deep unhappiness. (Maureen)

Students also demanded different teaching styles. Girls 'resented the strictness and rigidness' (Edward). Charlotte 'made the girls cry. I was too aggressive'. The boys demanded a confrontational style, viewing Edward's approach as 'soft'. Edward's small stature

> ... added to their lack of acceptance of me. Teenagers see maleness as being brash and macho and extrovert, exuding confidence ... I didn't do it very well. Therefore I lost face in their eyes. I represent something that doesn't fit what they think is ideal, who was fair game for anything they cared to throw. This was the cause of the stress I couldn't get round. Having to stereotype myself was against my personality.

Poor communication systems

Teachers described their schools as having poor communication systems and individual teachers as 'poor communicators' (Jonathon), with senior management teams having less contact with chalk-face staff. 'The head, we never see him' (Alex). Management was unable to deal with interpersonal conflict so avoided direct communication. 'Death by Memo', a major bullying management communication style (NASUWT, 1996), was a common tactic. Jessica described the fear surrounding the 'brown envelope in the pigeon-hole', the impersonal, critical memo that often contained threats to the teacher self, negative comments about teaching skills, possible official and unofficial proceedings, or additional responsibilities:

> If you get a brown envelope, that is it! Your heart sinks into your boots. You start shaking. You wonder what the hell's in it. Your whole world just collapses. You have to go into the loo to open it, your knees shaking, your head in the bowl. If you breathe in the wrong place, you get a brown envelope. It's like victimisation. That's how we feel in the place ... I never got a negative brown envelope. They still had the same effect on me as on others. Whenever Donald (headteacher) was gunning for another member of staff, you always felt 'there but for the grace of God go I – who's next?'

Extensive balkanisation of departments and competition in the marketplace reduced communication further (Hargreaves, 1994). The learning community had contracted.

> In the last four or five years, there's been a reduction in the amount people communicate across departments, across schools, a lot of dis-communication. The competitive structure creates more stress because you're competing with George down the road whom you used to chat to, discuss ideas with. It's become 'we don't want to talk to them because they're going to steal our students'. (Jonathon)

There was no arena for safe disclosure, discussion of school issues, or talking about feelings. 'Some people are really quite unhappy about the decisions being made. What we haven't really developed well is the ability for them to just say that, a forum' (Yvonne). 'If you made a comment in a staff meeting, you'd be asked to go outside and discuss it with Donald. People are not prepared to express their views at all' (Jessica). Schools were perceived as not good at asking appropriate questions or listening to staff. 'You were crying into the wind. You were trying to point things out to people, and they just weren't listening' (Maureen). At Walton Green, for example, Jonathon believed communication had 'broken down. Divide and conquer, dividing departments, dividing staff.' Terence's (a Deputy Head) Head rarely spoke to him, stopped inviting him to senior management team meetings, and changed the school layout. 'I was moved away from the administration area to an area that was created by the dining hall, one of the worst places to work'.

Autocratic decision-making

Teachers described losses in autonomous decision-making. They talked of 'repressive regimes' (Celia), 'a fascist regime' (Sally), 'a Judas mentality' where staff felt 'threatened' (Yvonne). Within the wider scheme of things, schools had lost power. 'We're at a watershed where external things have taken over the running of the school' (Jonathon). 'Schools [are] no longer the driving force, the vehicle. The driving force was local or central government' (Terence). 'We used to get involved in writing development plans. We've lost ownership. That's a downwards stressing, a depressing feeling' (Jonathon). In the schools, change was managed through autocratic leadership. At Walton Green, teachers reported 'downright dictatorship' (Alex), 'the modern breed of Head! .... democratic dictatorship. ... Because of the structures within the school, you find it very difficult to influence decisions' (Jonathon). Teachers described ineffective problem-solving. 'The problem is the system, too *laissez-faire*, not challenging, upper management not grappling with issues that need grappling with' (Alex). Much contrived collegiality (Hargreaves, 1994) was reported:

> It's: 'Let's have a brainstorming session', then in half an hour, you're told what to do. That frustrates me. I expect even-handedness. I was supposed to be contributing in creating the process, but I'm wasting my time because they've already made their decision. (Alex)

The introduction of the National Curriculum impacted even more negatively on those whose subjects were deemed outside its remit. As Head of Business Studies, Jonathon, for example, found it 'very difficult to influence decisions and things that are going on, being in a marginal subject outside the curriculum'. For Charlotte 'teaching drama didn't give me much authority to say anything. It's only a 'doss' subject. What do you know about anything? I've got no voice'.

Teachers found themselves compelled without consultation to abandon their successful activities. Being deprived of upper school work left Terence feeling 'grieved', and the further loss of timetabling and control within curriculum and pastoral elements 'a considerable disappointment, but there was nothing I could do about it'. Residentials were positive emotional experiences for Jessica, but her HoD prohibited her continuing them. 'I *loved* taking them out, got a tremendous amount out of seeing the kids develop. Their sense of achievement was my sense of achievement'. 'I loved having sixth-formers as students, one of my saving graces ... It was another nail in my coffin' (Maureen).

Surveillance increased, and became oppressive:

> Patricia was always in your room ... to keep an eye on us, check what we were teaching, check kids weren't misbehaving, check we weren't undermining anyone's authority .... You didn't dare speak to the technician, because you'd get told off. You felt as though you couldn't have a relationship with a member of staff. (Jessica)

Terence perceived

> ... people checking up on me, the school secretary timing my movements – what time I arrived in the car park, what time I got to my room, what time I left in the evenings, phone calls to see if I was in my office. I realised I could look out of my door and see her. When I lifted up the phone, I could see her putting down.

Bullying management styles

Bullying management styles were perceived by our teachers as a strategy to secure compliance. They felt a lack of 'fit' with the new educational regimes. Terence, for example, a deputy head in a city comprehensive, did not agree with 'the way the rest of the management team was going', and found that 'the atmosphere changed, became nasty'. Teachers described situations where one or two members of staff were singled out each year for abuse. 'The person who's being targeted at the moment is the union representative' (Jessica). As Goleman (1998) indicates, the observance of abusive behaviours meted out to those who voice organisational concerns, and the dismissal of colleagues, send clear signals to other members of staff – conform or be fired. Andrew felt targeted by his deputy head in the year he showed vulnerability owing to a combination of home and school circumstances. He and his wife Sarah described how the same colleague had in other years targeted other members of staff. Sarah likened the 'psychological pressures' used by management to 'an SS officer having sadistic vent on somebody, just pursuing it all the time, trying to eat away at his psyche'. Andrew felt 'in constant trepidation' of potential interactions with this man. 'It felt like being in the same room as a big hairy spider'.

Jessica described how cascade bullying affected the emotional climate of her department, where the Headteacher, Donald, targeted her Head of Department, Patricia:

> School's not a happy place. Donald has a reputation, certainly within the school, possibly the county, of having his teeth into somebody all the time ... a number of members of staff feel hounded out of their jobs. Once Donald gets his teeth into you, it's brown envelopes for everything. Patricia was getting brown envelopes every day ... Donald was bullying and blackmailing her but she was doing the same to other members of staff. She couldn't see the relationship between her behaviour and his behaviour.

She and her colleagues developed 'code signals. If we said to each other: 'It's an eggshell day', we would literally do anything to stay away from her, so we didn't have to come into contact with her at all'. Patricia reportedly 'hauled' Jessica 'out in front of a class and gave me a good telling off ... at departmental meetings, you're told off in front of colleagues'. In meetings, Terence was

> ... spoken down, told 'No, no, no'. Rather than saying exactly how I felt, I shut up, not prepared to pursue it because it just wasn't worth it because it was going to be criticised or condemned.

Maureen, helping a GCSE student working with boiling wax on one side of a partition, was '*ordered*' back into the teaching space by the Head who had just come into the lesson:

> 'You've left your students. I don't want parents thinking you've left your students'. The head was challenging me openly in front of students ... She was more concerned about how things looked when visitors came round.

Maureen was 'absolutely devastated because she'd wiped away any authority I had'. It affected her future:

> Planning was constrained ... It led to a gradual loss of confidence in my ability to cope in these situations, a general lack of happiness, exhausted at the end of the day, fearful of what the next day might bring, pretty joyless.

One of the rules in Sally's school, as in others, was 'Don't expose failings in discipline policies'. Because of her personnel skills, Sally was selected to advise other staff on classroom management. But her headteacher's behaviour towards her changed after she discussed perceived inadequacies in discipline policies in a school staff meeting, requesting their addition to the official agenda, and later wrote a letter on the subject to the Minister for Education. She found herself targeted, 'another threat, having to defend myself regularly':

> He kept zooming into my lessons, several occasions during that week, telling me off in front of the children. I knew what he was doing. Trying to catch me out, but they were good lessons, marvellous.

She spoke of him choosing to observe her

> ...'Achilles heel', unannounced, last period of the day, the most difficult class, renowned for disruptive behaviour. They come in high from their previous lesson where they're really bad, virtually impossible to settle down. It's hell ... I thought: 'Oh, my God, he's going to start on me! It's making me ill, more vulnerable, pains in my chest, neck, arms. If I put up with much more, I'm going to flip. I've got to leave'. When they start that game, that's it.

Negative Emotional Climates

Such regimes were characterised by negative emotional climates (see also Ball, 1987; Hargreaves, 1994; Beatty, 1999; Troman and Woods, 2001):

> It's very sad to work there. People are frazzled. There's a tenseness, a horridness about it, no happiness apart from a few friends I've known for years. There's nobody trying to make it a staff that gels together. It's the opposite, how not to run any establishment. Nobody should run their business like this. [Our headteacher] just makes people feel uncomfortable working there. (Margot)

These climates were marked by fear, lack of trust, blame, low respect, and chronic anxiety.

Climates of fear

Teachers reported 'rule by fear' (Jessica).

> ... making people ill. They only need a 'little thing' like divorce to crack up because they can't use their job to switch off ... Senior management [are] frightened to death of the Head. The Head's frightened. He's not doing as well as he thinks. (Sally)

These teachers feared some of their pupils, 'children approaching six feet, built accordingly and haven't got control' (Ralph), 'staff and students, frightened by child bullies' (Sally).

Changes in job security threatened their personal security (Milne, 1998). The imposition of the National Curriculum led to falling numbers in the subject areas (languages, arts, business) of some of these teachers. One common management strategy was to offset financial deficits by means of redundancies, temporary contracts, and employing cheaper NQTs. The threat of redundancy was

> ... frightening. ... For five or six years I've been trying to keep a department together. That's a strain and stress, the pressure to keep everyone in a job. You're fighting all the time. If students don't choose my subject, I don't have students to teach. That's my job, my livelihood, at risk. (Jonathon)

Fear led to closed cultures, 'too much secrecy' (Andrew), 'a lot of whispering behind closed doors, part of the fear thing' (Jonathon). 'Everybody stopped talking, just closed down' (Alex). Teachers felt 'very insecure, very threatened. You didn't become creative. You didn't become inventive. It stifled that' (Jessica). Post-Ofsted questionnaires were not answered honestly. 'Staff are frightened that if they fill in these questionnaires, they'll be found out. Then Donald [headteacher] will get his teeth into them' (Jessica). Fear 'disempowered' (Ralph) teaching communities, inhibiting creativity and stress management and reducing opportunities for developing open communication and active problem solving:

> You've got to be willing to admit that things are going wrong or there are problems, otherwise you'll never get them solved, but we live in a culture where so many people want to close the doors and hide things away because they're frightened. (Jonathon)

Climates of low trust

Changing trust relationships created stress for teachers through Ofsted initiatives, surveillance, hyper-accountability, insensitive monitoring and appraisal, the 'witch-hunt for incompetent teachers' (Sally), 'identifying failings in everybody ... sitting in classrooms, ticking sheets, no feedback' (Jonathon). Teachers lost trust in colleagues. Jessica, for example, was 'always thinking there'd be an ulterior motive'.

> Very few people keep confidences in our job. It's not part of their nature. They're not good at it. However sympathetic most people are, if they're anywhere near the top, it's going to go back to someone else. (Jonathon)

The climate of suspicion inhibited the development of empathy and active support-seeking:

> People hide their difficulties with students, not willing to admit to problems, their own inadequacies, particular issues in school they see as a problem, unwilling to trust someone to help them because they feel it will reflect badly on them. (Jonathon)

It also encouraged the formation of collective coping strategies such as social and psychological withdrawal, 'not playing the team game', which was 'not necessarily good for everyone else around them' (Alex) and further exacerbated the negative emotional climate.

Climates of blame

> The feeling I have, and others have, it's not just me, there's constant trying to find fault, trying to put blame somewhere, rather than helping. There are a lot of people that do help, but management policy is not one of support. It's one of criticism and blame. (Andrew)

Policies of 'naming, blaming and shaming' (Troman, 1999) led the teachers in 'failing' schools (Sally, Celia, Rebecca) to feel

> ... publicly maligned. We're a bunch of criminals, totally incompetent, that's the attitude. It's: 'Get rid of the naughty old staff who were failing pupils'. I witnessed colleagues being got rid of by the new 'super-head'. No one looks around thinking it's hardly any wonder they can't cope. (Sally)

Climates of blame reduced the teachers' perceptions of having support. They viewed senior management as 'out of touch with what goes on in classrooms, forget the type of students that causes problems to individual teachers. It's not individual teachers' fault' (Jonathon). Attention was diverted from addressing organisational issues and focused instead on management and/or individual teachers and students. Consequently the teachers felt they carried blame for poor organisational management strategies. 'Because they can't deal with their problems and responsibility, they think: 'Who can we blame? We'll blame the teachers'' (Sally). Schools were perceived as unable to solve societal problems. 'The problems are behavioural problems. We will never raise standards of attainment while [their] behaviour means we can't teach them' (Sally). Alex felt 'staff blame students rather than ways of working'. As Charlotte exclaimed,

> How can they blame bloody 12 year olds for troubles at school? .... It's our fault for making Keith (a pupil with behavioural problems) into what he is. We're the next thing to parents. If we haven't sorted him out then how can we blame him?

Climates of disrespect

Teachers here frequently mentioned the lack of respect afforded teachers by students, parents, the media and government, and 'constantly being knocked in the press. Every day someone sticks a knife in, the perception of what teachers are, what the job is. [We've] gone down and down in people's estimation' (Edward). Personal relationships with particular colleagues were singled out as defined by a 'lack of any respect, lack of professionalism' (Terence). Some management strategies diminished the teachers' respect for the managers:

> You listen in the staffroom to a senior teacher talking to a HoD about this teacher, that teacher. It shouldn't happen, creates a bad atmosphere, turns staff off. In our environment many people don't respect senior management. For instance, a meeting last week, a senior teacher not good at timeline jobs, ended the meeting saying he was going to severely take people to task, give them a good telling to if they couldn't meet deadlines, couldn't do this, couldn't do that, real bullying he was. You don't respect them. (Jonathon)

Some of the teachers lost their self-respect. Edward for example,

> was fighting a great wall of apathy, antagonism in school. Discipline was getting worse. I felt I was losing status and self-respect having to send for someone else, who was younger, often less experienced than me, to sort it out. It was weakening my position. I felt in the eyes of many kids I was a laughing stock.

Climates of chronic anxiety

> We call them 'eggshell days'. If Patricia's (HoD) angry, she throws things, slams doors, bangs things down, storms around ... You can't speak to her. You don't speak to her, just stay out of the way, try and ignore it, but you know you're going to cop it at the end of the day. (Jessica)

Frequent emotional confrontations with colleagues and students filled these teachers' working lives with chronic anxiety, created partly by numerous demands on middle managers:

> At the back of a lot of my angst, kids interrupting lessons ... Other people who couldn't cope with their own classes created stress for me. I spent too much time solving other people's problems, not concentrating on my own. (Ralph)

Teachers felt 'dread going in the staff room ... You're only going to get picked up for some paper you haven't filled in' (Charlotte). Ralph felt 'lucky' to get

> ... beyond the staff room door. Somebody would give me a piece of paper, or 'Guess what one of yours did yesterday?' as if they were actually mine, personal offspring. I'd be answering kids' questions at the door. So I would never rest.

Negative emotional climates were perceived as directly affecting the onset of stress-related illness and burnout. 'I'd become very introspective. I think it was just this dread, almost building one's mental inner self defence for the battle. That was what affected my blood pressure' (Gareth).

Low Levels of Emotional Literacy

The negative emotional climates engendered low levels of emotional literacy. Schools are highly emotional arenas, where the 'management and mobilisation of emotions are pivotal to the ways organisational order is achieved and undone' (Fineman, 1993: 1). Managing emotions well aids management, teacher development and teaching (Hargreaves, 1998b). This involves not only the capacity to manage anger, frustration, anxiety and sadness, but also mobilising emotions such as enthusiasm and joy. It also takes in the avoidance of aggressive and destructive behaviours, and monitoring and dealing with criticism (Klein, 1997). However, when emotion is mismanaged, the result is increased tension and impaired cognition, which impedes constructive social relationships and undermines organisational performance (Goleman, 1998).

Teachers felt the real problems in their schools resulted not from 'incompetent teachers', but from a 'lack of skills in human relations' (Alex). This was perceived as largely due to the organisation's inability to handle social relationships surrounding the management of conflict, the suppression of emotion, and a lack of emotional awareness.

Managing conflict

Our teachers described colleagues as 'at loggerheads' (Jessica). 'What I don't like about teaching is the aggro within the staff' (Margot). Jonathon, for example, observed that poor conflict management was

> ... frightening to watch. In other business environments, things like that do happen, but they're more manageable. In our job there's not a lot of personnel management.

Jessica's case illustrates how psychological harm can be increased by ineffective internal grievance procedures. Jessica felt management action contributed to her ongoing emotional trauma over several years and failed to protect her from further harm. Although her grievances were upheld at a meeting with her Headteacher, Donald, and her union representative, discord with her HoD Patricia continued, and led to a second attempt to resolve it. 'I had to put it in writing. Patricia and I had to discuss the contents with Donald, the two of us plus him'. This face-to-face confrontation was traumatic:

> I was in a hell of a state. I didn't expect it to go that far. I was shaking by the time I'd finished. I was not prepared to keep on being blackmailed into doing what my head of department wanted me to do.

Jessica's exam classes, sixth form residential and work experience responsibilities were reinstated. But still the abuse continued. 'Donald theoretically agreed with me, supported me, but continued to let the situation go on'.

Suppression of emotion

The schools managed negative affect by suppressing emotional expression. Teacher emotion was not perceived as a social signal to a stressed institution, nor as an attempt to deal with loss and recover meaning. The expression of apparently unregulated emotion was interpreted as destructive, threatening the power of the leadership and countering managerial purposes.

The teachers felt there were implicit emotion rules that discouraged expression of emotion. One unspoken injunction in their schools was 'Don't express negative emotion in open forum'. The teachers perceived management as poor at dealing with criticism, which they often interpreted as a personal attack. 'Many heads feel their authority is being eroded' (Celia). The teachers openly communicated their perceptions of collective concerns in their schools, bringing the problems of stress, 'crisis-management' (Alex, Terence), inadequate provision for special needs (Emily, Charlotte) and 'cultures of indiscipline' (Sally) into open forum, exposing 'cracks in the system' (Celia), and 'conspiracies of silence' (Jonathon). By so doing, they become 'bullet-carriers' for organisational anxieties.

'Don't listen to the emotions of others' was another emotion rule they perceived as prevailing in their school. Displays of emotion deemed 'inappropriate', and the failure to adopt appropriate feelings, were looked on as individual failings. In Walton Green, for example, Margot's deputy head Yvonne judged Margot as 'highly strung, you know', implying that Margot's emotional expression exposed an individualised personality trait, rather than signalling organisational anxieties. Jonathon also 'regretted' showing 'strong emotions' in Walton Green. 'People say: 'Oh, he's at it again''. Thus was the label 'being emotional' used to individualise and discount individual and organisational emotion. Teachers perceived schools as managing emotion through 'abnormalisation' (Goffman, 1961), neutralising negative emotion by deviance labelling techniques (Turner, 1987). These teachers, labelled 'dinosaurs', felt isolated, 'a threat' (Emily), 'a whistle blower' (Jonathon), 'troublemakers' (Celia), 'a bunch of militants' (Sally), 'mavericks' (Celia, Alex, Sally, Emily). They were viewed as 'part of the problem, not a solution to the problems' (Gareth). Sally sums it up: ' People like me they hate. The shutters go down'.

Lack of emotional awareness

Teachers identified the suppression of emotional expression as inhibiting emotional awareness in their schools. They felt teaching communities had lost their capacity for reflexivity, their 'social radar', instead displaying 'empathy avoidance' and becoming 'tone deaf' to emotional signals (Goleman, 1998). 'Everybody's chasing their tail' said Jonathon. 'No-one noticed the little messes I get into. They're so absorbed in their own crises, they haven't time to notice my little crises' (Charlotte). Ralph felt 'they're so submerged in work they don't have time to see what's happening to other people until something goes wrong, something snaps, a member is taken ill, or hits a kid because they've finally lost their rag'. The 'first stage in effective stress management' (Crawford, 1997: 103) is recognising stress and this is both an individual and social process. But there was scant recognition at either individual or collective level. Low levels of organisational emotional awareness hampered early detection, empathy and therapeutic action. Teachers testified that they, their families and colleagues were slow to recognise the severity of their signals of distress until acute bodily failure compelled action. 'Unfortunately [recognition] tends to come too late. People have actually jumped off the cliff before they've got support' (Jonathon).

The management strategy of replacing 'the old guard' (Jessica) with people more amenable to new regimes of power, rather than providing training to enhance emotional skills, was commonly observed in the schools. In Castlerigg, for example, several staff left soon after the merger. Edward, however, resisted advice to take early retirement, wanting 'to be in control. I would not be pushed out. Although I hated it, I'd still go when I decided'. No help was offered for people to find alternative employment. There was no forum for discussing moving on in a positive way without 'losing face', and little organisational awareness or empathy about the emotional consequences of rejection. 'The Head feels she has to be ruthless, cut out the deadwood, but we're people! We're not bloody bits of deadwood!' (Charlotte).

Negative emotional climates and low levels of organisational emotional competences led to a sharp increase in emotional labour.

Increasing Emotional Labour

Emotional labour 'facilitates and regulates the expression of emotion in the public domain' (James, 1989: 15), and involves efforts to change the degree or quality of emotions or feelings (Hochschild, 1979). Our teachers experienced an escalation in emotional labour with both colleagues and students.

Emotional labour with colleagues

Luke, Alex, Jonathan and Stephen were initially enthusiastic reformers. But they experienced problems when they found themselves 'the focus of imposition' of educational reform on their colleagues. Luke, for example, who was responsible for introducing the National Curriculum Mathematics pilot, said,

> It was very hard to sell it to others in the faculty, who felt a sense of injustice at why had they got to start this. We had to report back to other faculties, what we'd done, how it all worked, which didn't work at all, because suddenly you got antagonism from colleagues as though you were telling them they had to do this. They're thinking it's not government any more. It's you telling them to do this.

When Jonathon tried to 'encourage everybody to take ownership of GNVQ', he perceived himself in a 'no-win situation' and his co-ordinating role 'the middle management kicking school – no real authority, no management structure to support'. Without management training, staff 'wobblies ... created anxieties'. Diffusing emotional encounters diminished teachers' feelings of confidence and competence:

> There's a lot of temperamental people ... When a member of staff came shouting at me because of his own anxiety, I'd no authority to placate him, say anything, except: 'I don't make the rules. This is what's going to happen. I'm sorry. I'm just the messenger. Don't shoot me'.

Alex quickly antagonised colleagues by trying to impose change too fast:

> Coming in with both barrels blazing, I've offended people. Put my foot in it so many times. People are challenging me, trying to put me down. This is my problem with the human relations side. I can't personally deal with other people's negativity, can't change one department to another with no resources. There's too few people like me wanting active open learning and developing self-esteem, too many others who have withdrawing coping strategies that aren't good for everyone else.

Just when teachers were managing both their own conflicts and those of others and needed support, they were shunned by colleagues. Luke, for example

> ... got a lot of flack. Being isolated was difficult to cope with. I didn't feel valued in terms of the job I was doing because everybody else didn't want to be involved in it. I didn't feel valued culturally as a teacher.

It became difficult to pursue 'any sort of personal relationship with staff' (Jonathon). Situational factors thus increased their feelings of depersonalisation and their loss of school support networks. Those with poor skills in people management unwittingly alienated colleagues, increasing tensions and reducing the 'numbers of teachers committed to reform' (Fullan, 1997). These teachers rapidly experienced burnout.

Emotional capital was further depleted by trying to give emotional support to stressed colleagues (Williams, 1998). It can be very demanding to do this, increasing one's own vulnerability to stress (Tilden and Gaylen, 1987). Managers who were unskilled in appraisal, monitoring and mentoring caused 'a great deal of grief' (Margot), which needed managing:

> If you've someone not good at it, doesn't know how to do it, she can do more harm than good. Brenda is not trained to understand people's needs. She'd do more criticism, wouldn't know how to praise a teacher. It wouldn't occur to her that young teachers need lots of encouragement. Last year, I watched young people not given the right guidelines, and collapse on me. I watched young teachers literally tear our department to pieces, the stress from them part of my stress load, coming to me saying: 'Please will you do something about it. She's got to be stopped'. (Margot)

The primary burden for emotional support fell on women teachers, as Ralph observed. 'I don't think there is enough of a situation whereby male staff are able to talk to males. It's still perceived as a sign of weakness ... I tend to go to one of my female colleagues'. Jessica became 'the go-between' between staff and Patricia, her head of department:

> I got their burdens as well. I spent quite a bit of time on the telephone at home. Counselling is perhaps too strong a word but you're listening to them, taking on board their worries.

Caring for colleagues caused much 'frustration':

> It was just going on and on and on. It gets depressing because you see it all as a vicious circle. It doesn't matter what we do. We can't stop it. You've got to moan to somebody else to get it off your chest so you don't feel quite as burdened but I didn't know what to do for these people ... because I was in the same situation myself. I eventually started saying: 'You must go to Georgia'. I actually *took* them to Georgia. (Jessica)

Emotional labour with students

Teachers reported that stressful emotional transactions with students increased.

Managing stressed students

Some pupils were 'less mature, have less experience, less knowledge' (Rebecca), and were 'demoralised .... angry underneath as well that they have not been given a better education .... having felt school had let them down' (Gareth's wife, Marjorie). They had 'low levels of self-awareness, lack of confidence and really low self-esteem' (Celia), 'no boundaries because they haven't worked any out for themselves' (Charlotte), and 'low levels of self-control' (Jonathon). They 'don't go with any rules' (Marcus). They 'couldn't behave, couldn't sit still ... shout out for your attention, make very loud verbal comments .... attention-seeking, throwing tantrums, wrecking instruments' (Celia). This impaired teachers' motivation. 'I know it's part of my job to keep them interested but there's a limited amount teachers can do. There's got to be some interest coming from the other end' (Maureen).

'Pressures to perform' (Gareth) induced by league tables and the pressures of the marketplace stressed the students and teachers, so leading to a 'naming and shaming' culture for pupils, 'a witch-hunt on the GCSE C/D grades. We've got to name them and shame them, try to get them to be Cs. I feel so sorry for the kids' (Jonathon). Rachel reported seeing 'so many youngsters in a mad panic'. Academic pressures increased the emotion work for teachers. 'You need someone there who can calm them down' (Rachel). As Ralph asked, 'Do they create the stress, or do we create stress for them? It must induce some form of stress in them, which in turn induces stress in us'.

The National Curriculum restricted the variety of learning styles teachers could offer, forcing teachers and children into rigid ways of working, even though 'not all pupils learn in the same ways' (Jonathon). Pupils were 'not happy.... forced to go to this trough, but you can't make the bloody horse drink' (Charlotte). Jonathon felt that students who were forced into 'alien academic structures' were 'turned off education, the trouble being we're on that treadmill. A lot of them get switched off too quickly ... kids voting with their feet .... 20% absenteeism which is frightening'.

Managing challenging students

Twelve interviewees experienced problems with EBD children in mixed ability classes, finding 'behaviour patterns a lot harder to handle, the percentage of these students within a group getting greater' (Maureen). School was 'like a lunatic asylum. We're bombarded with rudeness from every direction' (Sally). Teachers highlighted 'the lunacy some children operate under, the dramas, huge numbers of statemented children. It's more and more like a battleground' (Rebecca).

Margot, Stephen, Sally, Celia and Charlotte all taught large numbers of children across the school, and GCSE to the full ability range. Music, art, and drama were chosen by many of the children with special needs who needed 'one-to-one attention' (Margot). Teachers reported being allowed too little directed time with special educational needs staff. Margot, who had 'a huge rate of success from very low ability kids, some of the worst kids in school, probably the only GCSE they'll get', felt that managing these students was 'where it's falling down, the behavioural problems. You only need one or two who are really barmy, where you can't get through to them'. Others had similar difficulties. They found mixed ability teaching 'frustrating. In a typical class, you've got ones who can barely write and geniuses. You don't have a chance to give them what they need' (Rebecca). So much emotional energy was required:

> To get a class in, attentive, quiet, the ones who throw things, kick things, bouncing balls, throwing pencils, ripping up each other's books, was twenty minutes, strategically arrange all of them, so this one wasn't next to that one. Within an hour, there were so many different difficult things – prevent a fight breaking out, stop them routing a little less able boy, one child would have a panic attack, one child's hearing aid would stop working ... all of which you were trying to sort out, yet trying simultaneously to teach them. (Rebecca)

Marcus explained his frustration thus. He was

> ... a highly qualified, highly paid professional, paid for teaching French to people who were never going to learn French. These kids can't read and write on their own. When you reached their ceiling, it was very frustrating for them.

Managing aggressive students

> It's a hard school. We've kids running in and out of classrooms, smashing windows. I'm trying to teach, have to go out. The toilet roll is on fire. They've kicked the u-bend off the sink. It's flooding the toilets. They've smashed the mirrors. There are children chucking water bombs around, pushing people down stairs. (Sally)

> They're setting off fire alarms, stealing, having fights, pulling people out of other classes, visiting each other, holes punched in walls, departments getting ransacked, computers messed up, graffiti, litter everywhere. (Charlotte)

The emotional climates in some schools were seen as increasingly governed by particular pupils' behaviour, creating stress for teachers and other pupils:

> The needy ones cry out for attention. I'm forced for the sake of everybody to deal with them first. If they didn't think that you were taking any notice, they started wrecking things. (Celia)

In Castlerigg, for example, Maureen observed how 'loss of control' became 'more widespread'. Edward offered this analysis:

> Somehow, between the boys and the girls, and the two different philosophies of dealing with students, emerged a space in which troublesome kids could operate. The worst of both worlds emerged. Students exploited the differences, playing off one kind of teaching against another, playing off individual teachers against each other ... The disruptive ones have created almost a way of life in the school now.

Dealing with children who had low emotional competences was outside the experience of many of these teachers. Marcus, for example, who had no specialist training nor any special needs assistance, experienced

> ... a big mental shock, having managed for 20 years to control children, and therefore educate them, I suddenly couldn't. The first time ever I'd had discipline problems. Once a day I was out of control.

Marcus had a reputation as a 'disciplinarian', and it was important for him to have power over his pupils (Blase and Anderson, 1995). But his students controlled the emotional climate in his classroom as he met aggression with aggression, his anger

> ... having no effect. The red mist coming over me, so I felt out of control. That made me angrier, shaking with anger, such a strong emotion. My vision would blur, I was so taut with anger. There was a need to dominate the kid because he'd done something I couldn't accept. He probably didn't know why I couldn't accept it. That was the frustrating part. They didn't understand they'd done anything wrong.

Student emotion, like teacher emotion, was managed here by abnormalising the students, designating them as 'loopy, sods' (Sally), 'leftovers' (Rebecca), 'lunatics' (Jonathon), 'nutcases' (Margot), 'grots, barmy as fuck' (Charlotte), 'immoral' (Edward), 'little oiks, rabble, little shits' (Marcus).

Changes in curriculum, inclusion policies and management responses to dealing with children with special needs, meant the nature of the pupils altered, 'new lads coming through, permanent exclusion from elsewhere' (Alex). This caused teachers to feel they were losing control over the emotional climate in the classroom, so adding to feelings of personal failure. Marcus for example,

> couldn't win with these pupils ...There didn't seem any logic in the way they behaved, mentally aggressive towards one another, not predictable in how they're going to react ... I felt it was my fault, something lacking in me.

'Students' views had prevailed and I had fallen' (Gareth).

Managing abusive students

Both teachers and pupils experienced threats to their personal safety from distressed children. Seven of the teachers said that abuse from students directly precipitated their stress-related illness. Emily felt 'definitely bullied' after enduring a 'beastly hate campaign. Two girls I'd clashed with engineered a revolt. Certain people actively took part, others enjoyed it vicariously'. Sally felt 'we're all abused all the time'. She spoke of an incident in which her colleague was 'hit by a sports bag thrown from the top window', after which spinal damage prevented her from working. Marcus described several recent painful incidents which had caused him to 'lose face'. In the first, an 11-year-old's obscenities provoked him to 'grab her by the ear, march her out of the room'. When her parent accused him of assault Marcus was forced by management to apologise to the girl and her mother, although 'the child was not expected to apologise to [him]'. Then he was physically threatened in a crowded school corridor by one student's boyfriend. The boyfriend was later made to apologise in the Head's study, but the many witnesses in the corridor 'just see him getting away with it. That's frustrating and demeaning, the type of thing I'm not happy about'. In a third incident, he was 'sent home in a state of shock' after a violent incident with a 'strongly built, butch-type 15 year old girl':

> I was teaching. The door burst open. She burst in, yelling to friends. I asked her to leave. She ignored me, carried on yelling as if I wasn't there. I took her by her jacket lapels, propelled her out of the room backwards until she got against a wall. She was f'ing and blinding, kicking, spitting. I lost my temper, kept hold of her, which meant I got head-butted.

Marcus, like many of our teachers, often perceived support from senior staff to be lacking:

> Confrontation in the past, I was always backed up, won the confrontation with help from a year tutor or headmaster. The incident was closed then for me. In recent times, the incident didn't close, preyed on my mind for long periods of time. (Marcus)

Women teachers talked of having to cope with what Emily described as 'constant sexual innuendo ... a lot of sexual harassment from 16-18 year old boys' that was not taken seriously by management:

> The Head said: 'Don't turn your back on them'. That was the support we got! ... locked into having to endure extremes of sexual harassment we found extremely hard. It's very difficult to tell a man what that feels like, the undermining, the impulse on boys and men to do it. The huge indignation you feel, that they don't see. They don't understand, think you're making a fuss about nothing, should shrug it off. You're a 'stroppy Women's Libber', rather than expressing something very profound. (Emily)

While on corridor patrol during morning break, Rebecca suffered a violent, unprovoked sexual assault by a 12-year-old boy with severe emotional and behavioural problems:

> It was painful. He came out from behind me, making direct eye contact with me, and walked down the stairs leering at me like a dirty old man, all the way down, as if to say: 'What are you going to do about it?' I just froze, couldn't believe it had happened.

Morag's breakdown was precipitated by 'this lad putting it about I'd been having it away with him in my room. I was terrified'. She claimed management had known about these accusations for some time, but had not informed her. No steps were taken to resolve the situation with the student. 'I just thought: 'Shit, that's it. Teaching up the swanney'. It was really a frightener. I handed my notice in'.

Teachers also became greatly distressed by students abusing other students. Sally, for example, witnessed a 'very serious assault' by a 15-year-old boy who punched a younger girl in the face hard several times. Sally intervened, 'holding on to this boy who was bigger than me... Saying to her friends: 'Keep her back, get her and follow us.' He was going to punch me, and stopped. He shoved me violently'. This incident 'tipped' Sally 'over the edge'. She had 'risked my life to save this girl'. When, still in a state of shock, she took her report in to the Head,

> 'Put it in my tray' was all he said. Five minutes later I was taking the register, still crying, then teaching all afternoon. The boy was still being rude to me, harassing me, accusing me of 'fingering' myself, three months later.

Teachers felt that the students' emotional problems were not addressed, causing severe problems for the teachers and for other students. Sending troubled students to year heads or senior management team members 'adversely affects standards of teaching and learning in their own work areas' (Sally). The teachers felt that school policies failed to meet the needs of such pupils. Gareth, for example,

> ... was left dealing with students whose problems and issues I just wasn't aware of. Nor was there any attempt to make me aware, to improve my skills. It was as if that part of things was no concern of mine, it didn't matter.

Directed time was not provided for middle management to manage such children, nor was managing student emotion dealt with collectively by the staff:

> The *real* cause of my stress was a hard core of about a dozen *real* problem characters. I sat down with a senior teacher and the Head. We identified them, the target list, but it was left to me to do the monitoring on my own. (Ralph)

Pastoral care was inadequate in the schools and effective action as rarely taken. Marcus's headbutter 'was back on the street walking past school as if nothing had happened' by the end of the same school day. Sally remained 'very upset about the outcome' of the most recent violent assault she had interrupted:

> We've let this girl down. We've also let the boy down. He's learned to punch women. God help any girl who crosses him. It's on file he's assaulted girls several times. He has a real problem, needs some kind of therapy. He was isolated for a few days. The children need to know we are not happy to have a boy who is going to be violent to them.

Rebecca felt that the boy who assaulted her was not given appropriate support. Feeling 'quite constrained by [her acting head's] reaction not to call the police', Rebecca 'wanted to get him assessed, get him to a psychologist'. However, specialist care was not forthcoming. Rebecca felt her school failed in its duty of care and did nothing to protect the boy from further harm. 'He was still in trouble. His behaviour continued. Eventually he was moved to another school, excluded over all sorts of other things after I left'.

Organisational discipline was no better. Punishments like suspension only exacerbated the problem, as the students came back worse than ever. 'If you can't get them right mentally, then you're up a gum tree' (Jonathon). Rebecca observed 'so many children slipping through the net, not diagnosed properly until it's almost too late to get help. They lose their bottle, lose confidence ... It's so neglected'. Teachers despaired of improving the children's emotional competences. Ralph, for example

> ... didn't see myself being able to bring about even minor changes. I found it dispiriting to be back at the beginning of term. You'd been making incremental progress all through term. They were learning to control their tempers, modifying their behaviour. But because there was no control at home during the vacation, it was a case of having to start all over again. That began to get me down.

Teachers felt that the need to maintain pupil numbers and protect the school's reputation led schools to conceal the problems they faced. They believed this compounded the schools' problems by preventing programmes being instituted that would enable students to understand and regulate their destructive impulses, manage conflict, build their emotional literacy and improve behaviour standards.

Emotional toil

> Teaching is hard emotional labour, often pleasurable, but always taxing, even in the best of times. (Hargreaves and Fullan, 1998: 60)

Teachers found that instead of demanding but pleasurable emotional labour, they endured burdensome and stressful emotional toil.

Despite their initial enthusiasm for many of the aspects of educational reform, our teachers found it difficult to manage their own growing resistance to the methods of implementation. Jonathon, for example, no longer 'fully believe[s] in the structure, the making of GNVQ. I wasn't happy with the product I was selling. It created a lot of internal strife'. Luke soon found the new mandates 'unwieldy' – that 'criteria based target setting... prescribed ways of working' and a 'tick box mentality', which did not sit well with his own values. 'It doesn't suit how my mind works. I don't think like that. I don't think you can expect children to think like that. I've never understood something has to be done by this age, that age'.

Secondly, management strategies that marginalised emotion increased the demands on the teachers to manage their own emotions. They were expected not only to curtail their emotional displays but also to adopt 'appropriate' feelings. But doing so requires the ability to separate elements of the multiple self in differing situations and the teachers reported that they no longer had the emotional capital to perform such tasks. However, as we have seen, they also contested the emotion rules dictating appropriate emotional expression. As Charlotte put it: 'Criticise my work, but don't criticise me. Tell me how to go on, how to do the job, but don't tell me how I've got to feel about it'.

Thirdly, the teachers tried to cope with 'frustrations' and 'fears of repercussions' (Maureen) by suppressing their emotion, donning an emotional mask to suppress their emotional pain (Hochschild, 1979, 1983) (see chapter 3). This further inhibited their levels of emotional awareness. Hope, such a constructive force in overcoming challenges and setbacks (Fullan, 1997), vanished. Charlotte talks about how she 'lost hope. I couldn't be angry and fight a war. What's the point of being a survivor when everybody else is in the water?'

In driving emotion underground, school management facilitated the growth of hostile subcultures that fed negative emotional climates, and reduced the teachers' capacity to rally positive feeling, to motivate and inspire their students. Management viewed the displays of emotion they deemed 'inappropriate' and what they saw as the teachers' failure to adopt appropriate feelings as individual failings. By suppressing teacher emotion, the schools destroyed a valuable signalling system which would shed light on school effectiveness and school health.

Conclusion

Negative emotional climates are typical of the new educational regime that is driven by the values of the market, competition, managerialism, heavy duty accountability, instrumentalism, technical-rationality, and that not only disregards, but is averse to, the part played by the emotions in teaching and learning. This chapter has shown how the consequences of such a discourse are played out in teachers' lives. To be sure, not all the consequences described here can be attributed to the new systems and to government pressures. Some factors, such as school mergers, are local and institutional matters; and some incidents reveal more than a touch of sheer 'bad' management. But the general effect of the new discourse in our teachers' schools was to create opposition to the humanist professionalism of the past, to destroy trust, to render communication impersonal, provoke competition among individuals and departments in the schools and eliminate collegiality, fostering cultures of blame, fear and guilt. The resultant hierarchical management and bullying, and the lack of emotional awareness are all typical and are well-attested in the literature (for example, Hargreaves, 1994; Menter *et al*, 1997; Helsby, 1999; Troman and Woods, 2001).

Gewirtz and Ball (2000) contrast what they call 'welfarist' headship and 'managerialist' headship. The former held sway from the 1960s to the early 1980s, and was characterised by dedication to a range of values which included caring, child-centredness, democratic participation, and 'collegiality, service, professionalism and fair-dealing' (Clarke and Newman, 1992, p.17, quoted in Gewirtz and Ball, 2000, p.255). These values clearly acknowledged the significant role played by the emotions in teaching and learning, though, while a prominent feature of teachers' practice, researchers have been slow to recognise this and the emotions have not received the attention in the literature that they warrant (Hargreaves, 1998a). Managers were socialised into caring values and how to implement them in practice. The 'welfarist' heads are, according to Gewirtz and Ball, fast disappearing thanks to 'early retirements of various kinds', and are being replaced by heads who are likely to be imbued with the values of the new managerialism.

> Further, for these new heads, 'good management involves the smooth and efficient implementation of aims set outside the school, within constraints also set outside the school. It is not the job of the new manager to question or criticise these aims and constraints' (*ibid*, p.255).

This shift has opened the gates to a 'stress cascade'. The managerialist discourse embodied in government policy and implemented without question through hierarchical management styles and negative emotional climates provide the ideal breeding ground for the stress 'virus' which 'feeds on itself', and where, if

> ... one person is unhappy, another person is unhappy. It spreads round within the community ... One stressed person is bad enough but when you get half a dozen stressed persons in that organisation, that's worse. That half dozen becomes a dozen. (Maureen)

Our teachers regarded it as possible to 'catch' stress, and to 'infect' others in a range of ways:

- from Government. 'Government constantly criticising teachers in general, criticisms from Inspectorates, Heads and Deputies under pressure from OFSTED, from the Government, passing it on to us. We're all feeling under more pressure than we did'. (Andrew)
- from managers: 'The pressures on Heads are tremendous' (Terence). 'The only reason the Head's behaving like this is because he's under stress (Sally)
- on to teachers: 'One of the causes of my depression is management pressures on me, a transfer of them through me' (Ralph). 'Colleagues tired, all stressed, sparking off each other, two very close inspections' (Rebecca)
- to pupils: 'It filters down through the school to pupils' (Rebecca). 'The way certain colleagues take their stress out on the children, the way they raise their voice, shout, scream creates stress for them which they then take out on other people' (Ralph)
- from pupils: 'very needy' (Celia), 'defensive ... They come with all that baggage' (Charlotte)
- and upwards from the pupils to the teachers and on towards management and government: 'I let senior staff know why I was under stress. I said: 'I need your help. I cannot control these kids and deliver the programme you need me to deliver. The atmosphere is just not conducive to this'' (Gareth). 'Writing to Blunkett, I panicked the Head, frightened the pants off him' (Sally).

For a significant number of our teachers, their stress cascaded further still – into their homes.

2

Origins of Stress 2: 'Eggshell Days' in the Home

> It was like walking on eggshells or a knife-edge:'If I do this, what's going to happen? If I do that, what's going to happen? Shall I just sit here? Do nothing? What are the rules?' I couldn't predict his reaction. (Ralph's wife, Gina)

According to Rowbotham (1973: 59) family relations were thought to function as 'a human alternative to the inhumanity of social relations at work', the private sphere being 'a place of sanctuary for all the hunted, jaded, exhausted sentiments out of place in commodity production'. The emotional stability of the workplace was conditional upon the family's ability to absorb emotional trauma, nourishing and returning its members to the public sphere refreshed. Women were expected to act as 'society's emotional sponges' (James, 1989: 24), soaking up workplace tension and providing 'emotional warmth and stability for the whole family ... good tension-free relationships between family members' (Oakley, 1974: 181).

However, the nuclear family as a haven that gave refuge and created warmth and harmony has been exposed as a myth (Elkind, 1994). The family is a potential site of emotional stability *and* emotional trauma, and traditional assumptions concerning the separation of working life and personal worlds have been challenged. As Kanter (1992: 284) points out, 'emotional attachments are not kept within bounds'. There is increasing evidence of 'spillover' effects (Rice, 1984) where 'stress arising from one sphere (family or employment) affects the other' (Ginn and Sandell, 1997: 420). According to Redwood (1998), 'stress in the classroom is a family affair'. Peter Lewis, founder of the helpline Concerned Spouses of Suffering Teachers

(COSST), is clear about spillover from school. 'The public should get some idea of the suffering in teachers' households. Believe me. It can be terrifying' (*ibid*). While good family relationships may ameliorate distress experienced at work, home arenas can also be significant contributors to work-related stress (Cooper and Davidson, 1987).

This chapter explores stress in teachers' home lives. We consider, first, the major stressors within the family; secondly, how the forms of stress spill over among work, home and other spheres; thirdly, how these emotional experiences affect family cultures and structures; and finally, the impact on family health and well-being.

Family Stressors

While new forms of work in the public sphere created new demands in schools, the teachers and their families continued to hold responsibilities for 'old' forms of work within their family spheres. When these were called in, the family domain too became a stressful arena, where demands exceeded resources because of the conflicting requirements of not only 'triple shifts' namely work, childcare and domestic tasks (Acker, 1994) – but also of elder and spousal care – a quadruple shift. Children, partners and elders competed for scarce 'quality time', itself a 'threatened form of personal capital' (Hochschild, 1997: 51):

> I'd a horrendous time for a couple of years ...You may be able to cope with [abuses in school] if you've no other problems, no other responsibilities. All these contribute to the whole picture. My grandmother's dying. An elderly friend is ill. I'm teaching all day, directing a big production. I'm racing over to the hospice. My father is ill, operated on. My mother, in her 70s, can't cope. My sister's cracked up. I remember leaving school, driving to the hospital, sitting with Dad, dealing with the awful things happening there. [During Ofsted] Dad caught MRSA (methicillin-resistant Staphylococcus aureus), died under horrendous circumstances. Ofsted I just didn't take much notice of, more important things to worry about, Dad on a ventilator. I was very close to him. I was in a hell of a state. Huge emotional trauma when he died, complaints to the hospital, Ombudsman's report, newspapers. (Sally)

Rachel's 'family problems made life so difficult that coping at school got out of hand'. Death and dying, healthcare, and family-related issues are among the major five themes in the most stressful life events (Van Eck *et al*, 1998; Van Someren, 1998). The main themes among our teachers were managing loss, managing chronic illness, and managing the home shift.

Managing loss

The loss of important personal relationships is a crucial factor precipitating emotional breakdown (Westman and Vinokur, 1998). In the build-up to breakdown, Alex, William, Rachel, Maureen, Sally, Edward and Marcus experienced the deaths of parents, close friends or colleagues. The deaths of both parents within two years profoundly affected Alex. 'When Mum died, that's when I really shifted about. Used to think of my own mortality, living day-for-day, *carpe diem*'. The death of a parent can cause past grievances, guilt and shame to surface. Rachel, for example, found 'it all came to a head when Dad died. I did respect him enormously, respected his mind. When he died, the anger bubbled out. That was part of my grieving'.

For Luke, Alex, Morag, Celia, Emily, Charlotte and Marcus, relationship break-up threatened their emotional stability. Luke was 'devastated, extremely angry, then frightened of how I'd behave – not violent towards anybody, violent towards objects'. Alex's Ofsted inspection for example, coincided with confirmation that his partner Paula was having an affair. 'I was in shreds, the anger swelling in me'. He was unable to complete his inspection week. Consumed with grief after the break-up, he became engrossed in finding ways of punishing her.

Teaching responsibilities did not allow time for grieving. Rachel, for instance, while grieving for her father, felt overwhelmed by work overload, and the reliance on her of colleagues and pupils to prepare materials and introduce GNVQ. Grieving was suppressed, pushed into the 'bottom drawer', often to resurface later (see chapter 3). 'It was put away. I didn't accept a grieving process at the end of that relationship, didn't talk about Angie to people' (Luke).

Without the domestic and emotional services of partners, Luke and Alex each became increasingly unable to cope with the activities of daily living. Alex stopped dealing with personal care, such as eating, washing and shaving, while Luke

> ... didn't enjoy going home. My home environment got really messy. I didn't bother doing ironing, washing, couldn't be bothered to wash pots. I was living like a pig, didn't see it as a mess. That's how it was for 12 months, gradually building up. I'd actually take days off work to tidy up.

The conflicting needs resulting from family breakdown caused emotional turmoil. Emily and Celia endured financial hardship after their divorces. For four years before her breakdown, Emily fought an unpleasant and costly battle through the courts for financial settlement. In the cases of Celia, Marcus and Emily, marital break-up meant having to manage the long-term emotional distress of their children.

> I have to be around for Angus. He finds life hard. He's still very emotionally dependent on me, never been easy, always had a big chip on his shoulder about his situation, always felt hard-done-by. Life is never fair. (Celia)

Three months before Celia's breakdown,

> Angus's father invited him to live with him for a year abroad. That threw Angus into trauma, threw me into trauma. He can't sleep at night. He cries. That's another thing we're working through.

Managing chronic and terminal illness

Families feel a moral obligation to care for ill family members (Radley, 1994). 'My marriage vows are very important to me, that I was there to care for him in sickness and in health' (Rachel). 'It's the duty of the children to look after the parents' (William). 'That was my role. I was an only child' (Alex).

By caring, the teachers meant being alert to the needs of others, allowing time to talk and express feelings, giving of themselves, showing love, concern and empathy, anticipating emotions such as grief, anger, despair and frustration. Rachel's husband Matthew, a former teacher, had been unable to work for twelve years due to stress-related illness. Rachel felt responsible for his daily care, but financial need meant she had to return to teaching:

> Although I knew I needed to work, Matthew needed me at home. I was terribly torn. That was very difficult to cope with. In the back of

> my mind, even before he admitted it, I thought he might commit suicide. He needed me there just to keep him company.

Rachel was simultaneously coping with her teenagers Michael who suffered with depression, and Ruth who had unstable diabetes.

Chronic illness depleted emotional capital. William's wife Lindsey, diagnosed with severe ME (Myalgic Encephalomyelitis), was housebound for long spells. Hospital visits and the constant search for treatment were exhausting and traumatic. William felt unable to meet her demands for stimuli:

> She'd ask what was going on at school. It was like an inquisition, not meaningful discussion. I tended to resent it. Every time I went out I was expected to give full detailed accounts of everything said, everything done.

Attending to the needs of elders demanded time and often required travelling to and from the parents' homes. For six months before her breakdown, Rachel made a 250 mile round trip every fortnight to visit her dying father. Alex drove several hundred miles weekly between his home with Paula, the university and his parental home, supporting his mother through bereavement and caring for her in her final months with terminal cancer, virtually full time.

Family routines changed to encompass the daily requirements of frail parents, reducing time for other family and school tasks. Andrew's 'schedule was hectic' for five months after his father-in-law had a stroke: 'leaving straight from school. Returning home around 8.30 we'd have a quick meal. We ate more convenience foods. I'd sit in the hospital car park, marking work'. During this period, his mother-in-law, who had angina and had suffered minor heart attacks, was hospitalised several times with recurrent nosebleeds. Three years before William's breakdown, his father died of cancer. His mother also developed cancer and became very demanding. 'I had to keep an eye on her, check she was eating properly. That took a lot of time'. His wife Lindsey described how his mother manipulated both her sons emotionally, undermining William's confidence and self-esteem:

> If he didn't see her daily, when he next went, she'd say: 'I'm more important than school'. She'd say: 'Good teachers never bring work

> home. Your dad never did, so you shouldn't'. Before Ofsted, she had to go into a nursing home. Somebody had to tell her she was never going home. It had to be William. She refused to speak to him again.

When a member of the family became ill, they could no longer be supportive. Rachel's husband Matthew, for example, 'wasn't able to help the family, to support us, causing problems, quite paranoid, depressed. He went on Prozac. It was at that point I started not to cope'.

Those who were well incurred extra duties. William's mother, for example, expected her two sons to provide total emotional and physical care:

> They had two years of virtually going every day. She didn't want Social Services, didn't want anybody in. The family will do it. She expected the garden kept, housework done, expected you to go talk to her. (William's wife, Lindsey)

William was the only male in this sample to take the responsibility for home care. With three teenaged children, caring for his wife and mother, and running the home, he had no time for himself. 'He'd got rather a lot on his plate!' (Lindsey).

These teachers perceived their schools as largely unsympathetic to, and unsupportive of, the demands created by family illness. 'I felt, here was I, a teacher, working my guts out to help children, and *they* couldn't give me any help' (Rachel). Andrew's headteacher initially offered support when he was told about his family difficulties. But when Andrew got behind with his marking, he received a formal letter from school management telling him: 'Never again let your personal problems interfere with school work'.

Such responses made the teachers feel even more guilty over spending time and energy on family care, deemed by the teachers as 'no more than most middle-aged people have to cope with' (Andrew's wife, Sarah). Rachel felt

> almost blamed for having to cope with personal problems by colleagues at school. I was putting my job in jeopardy, almost as if I was too caring. I was made to feel guilty by some. I don't think they could understand ... If I'd been in an office job, I would've had a day off to

> take Matthew to a doctor. But because I'd got colleagues, I'd got children I had to be there for, I couldn't take the day off.

Managing home shifts

Many teachers find it increasingly difficult to balance the needs of work and family life (Wallace, 1997). The home/work interface presented severe problems to our teachers. They did not see their schools as 'family-friendly'. They viewed promotion as incompatible with family life. Terence's female headteacher told him: 'You can't be a successful head and be married with a family. You won't ever become a head because you're too committed to your family'.

Family schedules and fears for their children's safety outside the home burdened them as parents, 'taking them backwards and forwards to sport, band practice and scouts, because we didn't like them coming back late at night in the dark on their own' (Andrew). Families were

> ... needy. At weekends my twelve-year-old son, Angus, he wants me, and Calum, my three-year-old wants me, and Hector, my present husband, has this fantasy of us doing everything as a family! (Celia)

It was mainly the women who talked of the emotional work they expended on smoothing family relationships. Rachel's husband Matthew, for example, 'would scream and shout at the kids. I got to the point where I was feeling I had to protect the children all the time. It wasn't a physical battering. It was a mental one'.

Their children's problems created emotional trauma for them, as they struggled to come to terms with sexual orientation (Charlotte), attempted suicide (Rebecca), relationship breakdowns (Marcus, Stephen, Charlotte, Rebecca), and exam stress (Rachel, Ralph, Stephen, William, Jessica). Stress was directly transmitted as teachers empathised with the distress of their family members (Westman and Vinokur, 1998). Rachel's thirteen-year-old son Michael, for example, had 'dyslexic type problems, very, very bright, wasn't learning to read. The reaction we got was he's just a naughty little boy'. For several years before Rachel's breakdown, she and her husband fought recurrent battles with their local authority to have Michael assessed. The Dyslexia Association diagnosed Michael as 'discalculate, with the verbal reasoning of an eighteen year old'. She related how, 'before SATs, Michael got himself into such a state, diarrhoea and vomiting in the mornings, he literally couldn't get out of bed', the summer before her breakdown, and recalled how his self-esteem was

> ... going down and down and down. He'd said to me: 'Look Mummy, all I want to be is a normal little boy'. I remember that. It really hurt. I was suffering the pain Michael went through.

Apart from William, the male teachers who had partners did not talk about the pressures of coping with day-to-day home care. The burden of home shifts fell largely on women, and they talked about the difficulties of being primary carers and carrying the full domestic load. Conflicting cultural directives for women to achieve success in both maternal and occupational roles, created severe role conflict (Lewis and Cooper, 1983). Women teachers here thought that balancing work and home was less difficult for men, and that gendered caring regimes meaning male and female teachers leading

> ... completely different lives. There's a vast difference between men and women in school. Men seem to be able to cut off much better. It's just a job. They can go home and wind down because their wife has made dinner, or cleaned up, or is only doing a part-time job. The majority of the women I work with are full-timers, and it's hard for them, very hard. (Margot)

Several women joked about needing the services of a wife. Most husbands took little responsibility for domestic routines. 'I might wash-up, make tea, pack sandwiches for the next day ... It doesn't come naturally' (Jessica's husband, Frank). Margot perceived the change in domestic routines as contributing to the onset of her illness. 'I've always done all the shopping, housework. I got a cleaner to help share the load, but she dropped out last year, just before I started to feel ill'. Living in a small village, she was unable to replace that domestic labour.

Male teachers were viewed as unappreciative of female teachers' family responsibilities:

> A lot of men expect you won't mention that. They won't accommodate it, because they have wives that do it for them. Even if their wives work, they still expect their wives to do it for them (Celia).

'The Head's whole purpose revolves around school. He can't understand why other people don't feel like that' (Ralph's wife, Gina). Margot observed that male teachers had different conceptions of time:

> They can't even be bothered to turn up on time. At meetings, there have only been women in the room. I want to say: 'For God's, sake hurry up'. They haven't got to go home and make dinner. It's obvious they don't have to look after the kids.

Gendered childcare regimes caused conflict between partners. Celia, for example, 'resented' the invisibility of women's nurturing role:

> [Childcare/domestic work] is traditionally what women have done. For years I used to think why is it that, when two people are working, the man never does it? My husband's a university lecturer, under a lot of pressure, works very long hours. He's not physically there most of the day. Part of me thinks: 'Why can't we be equal partners? Why can't he do childcare?' He's not going to come home at 4 o'clock. I can have as many tantrums as I like. He'll just say: 'No, I'm not coming home'.

The women's ideas of gendered roles were slowly changing, and they perceived the men as retaining traditional ideals of role differentiation:

> I still haven't got him to acknowledge that was the case. A lot of men aren't programmed to see it's unfair. He can't see it, even now. So it's useless to argue. Until he can come to his own self-knowledge, you can't make people change faster than they want to. (Celia)

As their responsibilities within the home increased and their opportunities for positive emotional experiences declined, the home ceased to be the place for release of stress, as William's account well illustrates:

> Lindsey didn't want us to book up to go anywhere because we might not be able to go. Everything dried up. It was cutting off the release valves. I couldn't release stress anywhere, couldn't release it at home. I wasn't getting out anywhere, wasn't relaxing. I didn't have time to get to the allotment. The garden went. I was too tired. With parents dying, Lindsey going downhill, frustrated, and me having to look after her, I took my eye off a bit, shut myself off to protect myself, without realizing it.

Hochschild (1997) notes that employees facing conflicts brought on by work and home responsibilities may begin to view the workplace as a retreat from distress in the home. Work can be therapeutic, its effects mitigating stress from home lives (Lewis and Cooper, 1983):

> When I was in the classroom, everything was fine. That was my sanctuary. I was successful at what I was doing there. Probably the only place I felt valued at that particular time. That's where I was in control. (Luke)

Rachel described how she 'used to go to school to escape what was going on at home'. However, as the tensions of implementing government reform increased, 'school no longer functioned in this way' (Rachel). While family trauma caused much distress, 'it was much less than the other things' (Celia). The overwhelming majority of interviewees believed work stress triggered their emotional breakdown. As Margot declared:

> To a certain extent, working women are all going to find this sort of stress [in the home], but it was manageable until this stress at work. The burden of work was being made too much to bear.

As home and school both became sites of emotional trauma, family health suffered as emotional distress spilled across the spheres.

Spillover

> For my kids, my husband, they were eggshell days. They were thinking: 'Oh God! What's she going to come home like?' When I did come home, it was: 'Get out the way!' The kids used to go into their rooms, probably stuff cotton wool in their ears while I exploded! (Jessica)

Teachers and their families reported that stress spilled over from school on to the home, and vice versa. Their analysis of their home and working lives demonstrates the interdependence of the two spheres. 'Clearly my stress was work-related and obviously the relationship had affected my work' (Alex).

School stressors colonising the home

Work colonised family time, the stress creating emotional tension through indirect transmission (Westman and Vinokur, 1998). The teachers' ability to separate the spheres, a key tenet of stress management, was impaired. 'I'd wake up in the night thinking about the job so I was separating out a lot less' (Marcus). 'It was difficult to cut off. At what point I lost that ability I don't know. At one stage I was quite good at forgetting about work' (Rachel). They recalled 'bringing too much of other people's burdens home' (Margot). Terence 'used to come home feeling very depressed. Argue more than I needed. My wife took the brunt of it'. Jessica's husband Frank recalled how 'getting knocked at school' affected Jessica's 'whole outlook on life. She wasn't in a position to bite back at school, the natural human reaction. It has to come out some way, bites at the people around you, the family'. Celia found it 'very emotionally draining. You end up pushing stuff inside yourself. You never shout at pupils, or are angry. You're always ultra patient and it was coming out at home'.

Home stressors colonising the school

The quality of emotional transactions outside school plays a significant role in teachers' wellbeing at work and has 'a serious impact on the performance and morale of a teacher at school' (Teachers Benevolent Fund, 2000: 19). Rachel recalled that her son

> ... Michael wasn't getting the help he needed. Before I went into school Matthew would open letters about this. He'd say to me: 'Look at this. They said this won't happen, that won't happen. What are we going to do about it? I think we should do so and so, and so and so'. I would be panicking about this. I'd be preparing to go to school, thinking I can't cope with this. Gripped before I went into school, the old adrenaline going boom, boom, boom, boom, boom, boom, boom, boom, boom, boom. I didn't have enough time to come down, calm myself, before I was getting BOOM, BOOM, BOOM from the kids. I didn't have what I'd call fighting mode. By the time I got into school the next stage set in. I didn't have the adrenalin to cope with these kids. I was yo-yo-ing from the adrenalin. That went on all through summer term.

Family health problems invaded the classroom literally for William, as his wife Lindsey, who taught in the same school, suffered frequent attacks of illness at school. 'She would just go dizzy, and completely pass out. I was called out of class, having to sort it out'. Chronic high emotional states impeded teachers' ability to respond to the emotional demands of teaching. Jonathon remembered 'shouting at the kids. I felt sorry for that. You go into school so uptight, carrying so much baggage that the kids suffer'.

Stress emotions colonising other spheres

Teachers and families reported stress contagion traversing multiple spheres. Margot's husband Stuart found worries about Margot intruded on his working life. 'It's always in the back of one's mind: 'I hope today's gone well. I hope Margot hasn't done anything stupid, that nothing's happened". Pauline, teaching in the same school as her husband Marcus, twice carried her 'eggshells' to school and 'erupted in floods of tears':

> It was a way of expressing my anger that this should happen. I knew [Marcus' illness] was because of some kids. In a subconscious way I might have been taking it out on the ones I had in front of me, asserting my authority.

Teacher stress traversed connecting spheres which contaminated other arenas. Frank, Jessica's husband, related how he created 'eggshell days' for employees in his management role in industry:

> My mind just wasn't on the job, pre-occupied. You're trying to concentrate. Inevitably you snap at people. I remember feeling guilty about it afterwards. Not when I did it. I wasn't conscious of it when I did it, but afterwards I thought: 'I didn't handle that very well'. Employees have a problem. When the boss is snapping at you, it's not so easy to snap back.

Frank feared that his unhappy staff carried his 'eggshells' home and so continued the cycle with their families.

Merging spillover effects

The family sphere became a 'holding environment' (Stapley, 1996) for stress from several working spheres, where both partners, and sometimes adult children, worked outside the home. For some families, the stress from two teaching careers merged (Stephen, Terence, Edward, William, Gareth, Marcus, Ralph, Alex). As Stephen relates, his own stress competed with that of his wife Jenny and his son Bobby:

> Jenny teaches in a special needs school. Her job is very stressful, these children very special, special ones! The rules there are changing all the time, more and more severe [cases]. [It's] very upsetting, with children having fits etc frequently. Occasionally you get a death. Bobby worked terrific hours. Gone by 5.30 a.m., not back until midnight, the same the

> next day, travelling all over the country. We were concerned about his well-being. Absolutely nothing was going right for him.

Andrew's wife Sarah explained how her 'eggshell' emotion, built up in her work in the health service, colonised their home:

> I was having extra pressure at the hospital. You always felt watched. My boss was always asking me to work faster. The stress had got to him. He was relaying it, without realising it, on to other people. Everybody there is overworked and stressed. It's a thing in public services. You have this sense of, not necessarily bullying in the strongest sense, but it goes down the line each layer. I didn't feel like going. I got butterflies. I was getting upset. I talk about everything I feel to Andrew. Tell him if I'm upset, if I'm annoyed. Women do. So Andrew was supporting me, helping me cope.

Teachers were thus called on to provide emotional support for partners and children at a time when their own coping resources were diminishing. Families were caught between spillover emotions from competing institutions, the home being a repository for stress emotions from several arenas. These threatened family cultures and structures and the family's health.

Family Emotions

The families experienced negative emotional climates, changes in emotion work, and changes in key family emotional competences such as decision-making, empathy and communication patterns. These damaged family cultures and structures.

Emotional climate

The emotional climates in the teachers' homes became increasingly negative. 'Margot made everyone's life thoroughly miserable. The slightest word out of place and Boomph!!' (Stuart). To Frank, living with Jessica was 'like trying to walk through a minefield'. Teachers indirectly transmitted stress through disruptive behaviour. Maureen analysed her own changed behaviour as 'work control needs displaced onto the home environment. I thought I was losing control in one area [school]. I wanted it back in another [home]'. Jessica became 'fanatical about keeping things neat and tidy. I didn't want to start clearing up after the kids, making meals, wanting everything just so, [to] concentrate on schoolwork'. Jonathon took complete control of domestic routines, from keeping the fridge stocked to loading the washing machine, criticising Jo, who reported suffering verbally if she did not appear sufficiently grateful.

Seven families experienced lengthy periods where members vacillated between explosive outbursts and withdrawal. Ralph would 'regularly explode', displaying 'growing impatience, intolerance with everybody', 'little things blown out of all proportion' (Gina). He displayed 'classical aggression', becoming 'totally irascible, obsessive'. Gina likened his behaviour to a 'persecution complex, everything sent to try us'. As Ralph's obsessional behaviour intensified, their two children experienced the home atmosphere as 'scary'. Climates of fear ensued. Margot's behaviour swung between two extremes creating alarm:

> Initally it was total manic, then a cocoon effect. She was really not on this planet. This insular effect frightened the hell out of me! Her character is quite fiery. It [became] so flat and docile. That was frightening. Total reverse of character basically. (Stuart)

Threats to mental health caused anxiety:

> This is more frightening than most illness. If you cut your hand off, you don't sit here whittling. You do something very quickly. It wasn't easy to get her to do that. That's the problem. Medical things are easier to nail down. (Stuart)

Along with GPs, their partners tried to stop the teachers from returning to teaching too soon. 'My worry is it could slot back' (Stuart). In eight cases, these fears were realised.

The adoption of individualist stress discourses impacted negatively on family emotion leading to climates of blame and mistrust. Some partners knew little about emotional micropolitics and organisational stress (as discussed in chapter 2). Terence's wife Alicia, for example

> ... couldn't understand people could be so devastatingly cruel. I'd very little inkling of the politics within school. I felt terribly let down, very accusative, my first thoughts: 'What have you done wrong? Why couldn't you have sorted this out?' I could not be sympathetic. It was difficult to understand how he could just sit back and not fight it, having been such a fighter ... I lacked trust in what he was saying was true, felt his judgments must be wrong.

Family relationships suffered. Jessica and Frank's children, for example, became 'very annoyed, very resentful'. According to Jessica, 'Frank felt I was destroying the structure of the family'. Fiona described her father Ralph as

> ... snapping, blaming one person. Another person would start blaming the next person. It would go round and round ... Dad would say something to Mum. Mum would say something to me. I'd say something back to Mum. I'd stomp off upstairs. Paul would come down. Dad would say something to Paul. Paul would say something to Mum. Paul would stomp off up the stairs. Everyone with a frown on their face. He was so picky, you were caught between a rock and a hard place.

The home environment lost its function as a place of refuge and safety. Stuart told us how he

> ... didn't look forward to coming home. She was talking about it all the time, how bad it was. It was getting worse. I've heard it so many times before. I knew exactly as soon as I opened the door what I was going to be in for, blurting it all out, day after day.

Jessica reported her husband Frank 'wondering what mood I was going to come home in, dreading coming home. He thought it was going to be another moaning match from me. It does very badly affect your partner'.

Instead of providing a haven, the home increasingly became a site of tension and insecurity.

Emotional labour

Emotional labour within the family involves managing the 'interpersonal economy of domestic relationships' (Morgan, 1996: 131), which involves caring for and caring about family members, dealing with family well-being, health, illness, the body, its control and its maintenance, and smoothing interpersonal relationships. Margot's husband Stuart described the emotional labour involved as 'trying to juggle very many balls without dropping any, keeping the boys happy, keeping the job OK, trying to keep her talking'. He held his own feelings in, since 'blowing [his] top' might have 'pushed her over the top'.

Divisions of labour within the home were disrupted by spillover stress emotion. The teachers lost their abilities to contribute towards family care. 'I couldn't cope with normal things like ironing. Cooking dinner was a major task' (Margot). Jessica 'hadn't got time for the kids'. The loss of such labour increased demands on partners. Like other partners in this sample, Gina took over both her and Ralph's share of household responsibilities:

> Ralph's the chancellor. These things weren't getting done, normal everyday household jobs. I took over doing things I hadn't done since we were married, paying bills, sorting money out, driving the kids to school, the big shopping. I thought: 'This isn't my job – it's Ralph's', but for the sake of my sanity and peace and quiet, I was doing them. (Gina)

For Alicia and Terence,

> ... it was a time of financial crisis. Terence pushed things away. He'd spent so much time at the computer, preoccupied with what was going on, financial things, all sort of things in the home he hadn't been able to deal with, built up. I was very worried. The only option was I had to work fulltime. Terence was in a terrible state. We had to get out some special loan, not from the bank. Things were very much out of control. (Alicia)

Children took over tasks normally done by parents. 'The reason this house is clean is because my sons are cleaning it' (Margot). Her husband Stuart began cooking the evening meals. Ralph's daughter Fiona returned from school at lunchtimes to make him a meal, took over ironing his shirts, answering the telephone, and taking materials to school for him.

Teacher stress disrupted established support networks. Maureen, Charlotte, Rachel, Sally, Emily, William, Rebecca, Jessica, and Celia felt unable to support family members adequately. Maureen regretted having no time to care for her elderly aunt who was living with her. 'Jonathon felt very guilty that he couldn't provide for his mother, couldn't support her' (partner Jo). Jessica's husband Frank

> ... resented her spending so much time on school. She wasn't giving the amount of time she *should* have been spending *with* the family, *for* the family, not just doing jobs, just relaxing.

Gina

> ... felt down at the bottom of the priority heap. Ralph didn't want to know, didn't care about pleasing us, doing his best for us. He'd put headphones on, shut himself off.

As work encroached on family time, families became upset at losing quality time with the stressed parent. This involved extra emotional work, in what Hochschild (1997) refers to as the 'third shift', soothing children's and partners' feelings. The teachers who were mothers spoke of spending additional time and emotional resources calming distressed children, as Celia well illustrates:

> They were very confused by why Mummy was not working, why she kept crying. ... I tried not to think about them. It's too painful. I was too tired to relate to them nicely, grumpy, very cross. I wanted them to go to bed. I needed some space in the evenings. Children pick up these signals. That's when they have tantrums. They're more difficult when you're under stress, fight for your attention even more.

Family dynamics changed. Rachel, for example, after spending so many years providing care for her troubled family, became more irritable and intolerant of her children, 'less aware of me trying to do my best and more aware of what I wasn't doing' (daughter Hannah).

Families found it difficult to balance the emotional needs of two professionals seeking simultaneous emotional support. 'When we were both under lots of pressure, that was bad news' (Celia). 'I wanted to let go of it [teacher stress] and so did she, two teachers living together. We were arguing more and more' (Alex). 'We both had an awful lot on our plates, working more and more with very little time for each other, neither of us in a position to support the other' (Stephen).

A gender imbalance in emotional literacy was evident in some homes (Neustatter, 2000), some of the men finding it harder to manage their partner's stress emotions. Where both partners were employed full-time, couples experienced conflicts of interest. Like others in the study, Alex and Paula's concepts of support provision were mismatched. Alex acknowledged that he expected Paula to fill all his emotional and domestic needs:

> I was expecting her to be my Mum. She couldn't be. She knew things were going wrong but didn't know how to deal with it. I saw that as disloyalty. I remember saying to her: 'A job defines a man. It's important that I'm head of department by 40. I can't do with negativity. I can deal with it at work but I can't deal with it here. I need support'.

With the hindsight provided by counselling, Alex has realised that his conventional ideas of gender role divisions led him to expect to receive unconditional emotional support from Paula without providing similar emotional input for her. This, together with spillover overload, contributed to the breakup of the relationship. 'What I couldn't face was that I hadn't put as much into the relationship and that's why I got left'.

Emotional literacy

> Communication broke down, the straw that broke the camel's back. (Alicia)

Interviewees reported lowered levels of emotional literacy within the family detrimentally affecting the family's health. Families experienced losses in emotional awareness. 'I wasn't too tuned in' (Ralph). 'It was a slow process. When it reached crisis point, on reflection, I look back over probably two or three years, it's not been right' (Terence's wife, Alicia). 'A dear uncle died, Olivia's best friend died. Olivia had to carry her workload. She needed more support from me but I wasn't aware enough to give her that' (Edward). Familiarity with their partners and ignorance of stress-related illness reduced families' capacities to see early signs of danger. Lindsey, William's wife, was 'with him all the time and didn't notice. Good friends came round. They saw how bad he was, how he'd altered'.

> The only sign was he'd come home from work more tight in himself, more miserable, something deep going on. I knew he was fed up, really annoyed, but I didn't know he was getting ill. (Sarah, Andrew's wife)

Patterns of decision-making altered. Edward

> ... wasn't contributing to family decisions. They'd decided themselves because I wasn't willing to join in. Then I argued with the decision. So I was alienating myself from the family.

Levels of empathy declined. 'I was feeling really uptight, yet couldn't talk to Andrew about it. When I did there was no sympathy' (Andrew's wife Sarah). Ralph would ask his children how their day was, then not listen to their answers. 'The next three and a half hours, it was how was his day!' (daughter Fiona).

Communication was viewed as the most important emotional competence for family health. 'Gradually, you get out of the normal social communications to a much lower level' (Frank). 'The only time I managed to talk to him was in the car, because he'd come back in and work' (Gina). 'The boys started to disappear, tried to hide. You saw very little of them' (Stuart). Stress was transmitted indirectly by socially undermining communication patterns, 'displaying negative affect and negative evaluation of the person' (Westman and Vonikur, 1998: 140). This pattern is commonly exhibited by stressed couples and demonstrates the social nature of emotion. Partners were drawn into playing destructive emotional games, characterised by conflictual interaction styles (Stewart and Joines, 1987). Andrew and Sarah's discussion of their spiralling distress illustrates this clearly:

Sarah: I was just so irritated. He was putting these barriers up, not sharing it with me.

Andrew: Sometimes I'd get really angry. If I stormed out of the room, she might come after me. I'd keep going to the toilet. Lock the door!

Sarah: You were running away from interrogating. Tell me, tell me – nag, nag.

Andrew: I didn't want to tell you. I had to get away. I couldn't just leave. When you live with someone, there's nowhere you can escape to.

Sarah: You were getting more and more angry. I was getting more and more frustrated, and therefore I was getting angry.

Andrew: The more I denied there was anything wrong, the more you pumped me because there was something wrong. It was stalemate.

Transactions were frequently crossed, when partners had opposing aims in their conversations (*ibid*). Some of the partners adopted problem-solving approaches, opposing the distressed partner's effort to seek emotional support. Alicia, for example, would seek to further her understanding of events and processes by asking questions such as 'Why didn't you do this?', whereas Terence just wanted her to just listen.

Emotion rules

Although our bodies are the sites for emotions, it is primarily family relationships that provide the context for managing emotion (Morgan, 1996). In some teachers' homes, the rules on which these relationships were based were contested. As tensions grew, customary boundaries of emotion were disrupted. Matthew, Hector and Terence grew up in 'differentiated' families of origin, where emotional expression and open discussion was encouraged, whereas their respective partners Rachel, Celia and Alicia came from 'undifferentiated' families in which the expression of emotion was discouraged, disagreements signalling disloyalty (*ibid*). These discrepancies became more apparent as teacher stress colonised the home, leading to 'very interesting family dynamics, very explosive' (Celia).

The interpretation of emotional expression as a signal of distress was in some cases gendered, emotional expression for males tending to be viewed as a sign of physical illness. 'We thought he'd had a heart attack' (Fiona). Celia, Charlotte and Margot's partners all saw emotional expression as a sign of mental distress that would require psychiatric intervention. 'I was going up the wall. I remember Stuart saying at one stage when I was screaming: 'You need to see a psychiatrist. You really are ill', and I was' (Margot). It was mostly the men who viewed the home as a safe arena for expressing emotion:

> In the work environment I've never lost my temper. It transposed itself at home, a much more secure environment, freer. In the home environment, I don't have any problems. I will express anger, as will my family, but also express affection, care as well ... You've got that security. (Terence)

Terence's wife Alicia, however, disagreed. Feeling unable to express her emotion in the home, she cried on the way to her primary school. Providing a comfort zone for stressed teachers meant that their partners lost the opportunity to use the home as an arena for emotional release. Jo, also a primary teacher, stopped discussing 'school problems and burdens. It would just stress him out, seeing me getting stressed'. In her efforts to protect Marcus and colleagues, Pauline found herself without a support network:

> I tried to suppress it, worrying about the effect it had on people. If I didn't, colleagues are not going to do their job as well ... I didn't feel able to bring my concerns home. I couldn't talk about it because Marcus was going through the same thing but worse than me. It'd only make it worse for him. He'd be worrying about me worrying.

Gina's 'safety valve' was

> ...to dissolve into tears, my natural reaction. Ralph hates me crying. I mustn't let him know I'm crying. If he realised I'd got upset and cried, he'd have got ten times worse, blow his top quite literally.

Offloading their own stress tended to provoke rescue attempts from partners, as Marjorie explained:

> I have to be careful I don't moan too much about college. If I start moaning, it's: 'We've got to get you out of there'. I think: 'Whoops! That's not necessarily what I want'. That's harping back to Gareth's school when he was not happy.

New emotion rules thus created situations where partners felt forced to repress their own emotion, so increasing demands on their own emotion management and feeding family burnout.

Deterioration in Family Health

Stress 'crossover' (Bolger *et al*, 1989), 'where stress experienced in the workplace by an individual leads to stress being experienced by the individual's spouse at home' (Westman and Etzion, 1995: 169), was common in this sample. In his study of the impact of HIV/AIDS on the home lives of families, Ankrah (1991) found that family members experienced multidimensional burdens, overwhelming their psychological, emotional and spiritual needs. Positioning as unofficial health workers damaged the teachers' families. 'It affected Alicia quite a lot. She could see I was going downhill. I couldn't see what she could see' (Terence). Families experienced high emotional states, damage to family relationships, losses to family identity and burnout.

High emotional states

Families underwent huge emotional struggles as they came to terms with loss, insecurity and uncertainty. 'Dad was not the person I knew' (Fiona). Ralph's family felt 'confused', not knowing 'what on earth we'd done wrong. We wondered what we could do to do the right thing. There wasn't an answer. Whatever we did, it would have been wrong' (Gina). Stuart felt 'powerless':

> I could see the stress, could sympathise with it. I couldn't do much about it. I don't understand the school. The Headmaster knows all about it. They all know. What can I do? I can't tell the Headmaster how to run his school ... It's round the proverbial mulberry bush, totally frustrating because it was out of my hands.

Pauline felt 'helpless'. Sarah became 'resentful', 'in despair', as Andrew withdrew into a shell she couldn't break through. Feeling traps ensued as powerlessness led to 'shame. It doesn't make me too successful does it?' (Stuart). Their partners empathised with the teachers' distress and experienced their pain. The stress was directly transmitted through empathy. Sarah

> ... was in a state of shock. Our life had been so turned around. I felt absolutely furious they had done this, horrified, angry. I wanted to go down that school and wring their necks. I shouted, swore, declared absolute war on those people. I'm still angry they can do this and get away with it.

Gareth's wife Marjorie directed her anger towards the government, wanting 'to write to the Secretary for Education ... who was going on about teachers who can't control'. Two years later, she still felt 'hurt', and became tearful during the interview. The possible surfacing of negative emotion caused some partners to refuse interviews. Maureen's husband Graham, for example, who could be heard shouting 'Bloody Management!' from the next room during an interview,

> ... is a very sensitive person. What's happened to me over the last few years has been very painful for him, one of the reasons why he didn't want to be interviewed. He hasn't come to terms with himself, how it's affected me. (Maureen)

Damaged family relationships

There was long-term damage to family relationships. Frank wondered 'whether it will ever go back. It's gone and that's it. Our daughter Janice is more distant from us than she would otherwise have been'. Teacher stress invaded the bedroom. Efforts to catch up with work disturbed partners' sleeping patterns, and deprived them of sleep:

> Even if Ralph was in bed, he was reading well into the early hours. The light was on. I'm hopeless with late nights. I got to the point where I'd think: 'I can't cope with this'. (Gina)

Clinicians have linked problematic sexual functioning with emotional crises and major life stressors (Morokoff and Gilliland, 1993). Teachers and their partners reported a loss of interest in sex, ascribed partly to exhaustion. 'It goes to zero' (Ralph) through 'sheer tiredness ... although we do bump together occasionally' (Ralph's wife, Gina). Margot described sex as

> ... an absolute nonsense. You couldn't have sex if you're so shattered. Your whole way of life was ruined. I'd be asleep at 6, 7 o'clock sometimes, wake up, then be asleep again, and sleep all night.

Frank felt 'there never seemed to be a long enough period so Jessica could settle down and become reasonably happy so we could relax a little bit'. Alicia

> ... lost any interest in sex. It was not important that Terence was impotent. He wasn't coming to bed ... I can't just jump into bed and have things hunky-dory.

The loss of sexual relations fed into individuals' sense of bereavement and identity.

Loss of family identities

We derive much of our sense of self through transactions with others (Woods, 1992). The loss of positive social transactions threatened family members' identities. Partners became estranged from their familiar selves. Alicia, for example, saw Terence as performing a key role in defining her sense of self. She felt the loss of his emotional labour acutely:

> He's the one person I let my mask off with completely. I felt my batteries weren't being built up. I was trying to build myself up. Terence couldn't do that for me ... I was just not myself at all ... The whole thing had a catastrophic effect on my view of Terence, who he was or is. My world to some extent fell apart. This man had always been my brick wall. He'd always been the sort of person I looked up to.

Ralph's children observed their mother Gina losing her confidence. They described her as becoming 'a fidgety little mouse' who 'wasn't quite sure if she should belong here'. Stuart keenly felt the loss of Margot's emotional labour, which supported his sense of self. 'One of the attractions with her is she has a big personality of her own. I suppose that does me good. It keeps me in check. Else I tend to run away with things'.

Capacities to give and receive affection changed. By withdrawing from family interactions, some teachers were unable to accept support from partners, who then experienced the loss of their roles as confidante and supporter as a threat to their identity. 'I felt terribly wounded and excluded' (Alicia).

> If I'm upset, if I'm annoyed, I tell him. If I've a problem, I hope there's sympathy coming. Equally I want him to tell me so I can sympathise, but he wasn't telling me. I felt shut out. I thought: 'Why aren't you telling me? What am I here for if you're not telling me?' (Sarah)

Frank felt

> ... there was a definite change in the way Jessica was able to express affection. She'd not want me to comfort her. Push me away. That's difficult to come to terms with. The natural reaction if somebody's feeling hurt, you cuddle them, show your support. If you're being pushed away, it changes it from a family situation to an acquaintance.

This increased feelings of depersonalisation. 'I grew more distant' (Frank).

Family burnout

Partners reported interpersonal tension and personal distress suggestive of family burnout. Teacher ill health added to levels of emotional exhaustion. 'I was coming home at lunchtimes from school to see if he was all right. If you're on your own all day, and you're not feeling well, it's a long day' (Ralph's wife Gina). Gareth's wife Marjorie experienced difficulties concentrating on tasks to hand. 'I don't think I did as well in exams as I could have. The work was tough because of what was going on and I had to work harder as a result of it'. Gina, also a teacher, 'lost [her] sparkle', finding the experience influenced her own feelings of competence. 'I did get to the point of absolutely sheer tiredness, exhaustion, and when you get like that you can't think straight'.

Depression was common. Ralph suggested that Gina's depression three years earlier had been directly transmitted to her by him as 'the tension' he was experiencing due to 'management pressures' spilled into their home. Alex's partner Paula 'was getting more and more depressed'. Terence's wife Alicia 'lost [her] sense of humour ... got depressed'. Edward's wife Olivia was

> ... feeling more stressed, on medication for depression for eighteen months. A number of times she's said she'd like to give up her job but she couldn't because I was having it even worse. 'However bad it is, I've got to keep working', she'd say. That added to the depression.

At some point during the downward spiral Rachel's entire family took medication for depression. She felt her daughter Hannah's depression was caused partly by her inability to provide support while she was absent from school for a year at a time when her daughter experienced multiple problems. Ralph's children both experienced problems at school, Fiona doing less well in her GCSE's than expected.

In some families a burnout cycle evolved where the partner's burnout became another stressor for the teachers, adding to their own burnout (Westman and Etzion, 1995). Terence's wife Alicia is clear about how this happens. Highlighting the lack of support for stressed teachers and their families, she compared the isolation of stress with that of new parenthood:

> It's like when you have a baby. Your world is upside down. You meet with a group who share the same things. How much better it feels for you to share. Yet in this scenario, there was no support – no-one to talk to, no-one to ask. It was hard all round.

Experiencing depersonalisation in the home, she developed work and leisure interests outside the family to feed her identity needs. Her teaching became 'all-encompassing'. Starting 'evening classes of various sorts', she 'was out of the house much more' – which was only possible 'because Terence was looking after the children'. Her coping strategies included reducing negative emotion by hiding behind an emotion mask. 'Quite good at being outwardly OK, but inwardly suffering', she repressed her emotion, 'my coping-with mechanism to put this front up that everything was all right ... I couldn't reach out to other people'. She avoided socialising, aware she'd 'have to put [her] mask on when with other people', and this added to her feelings of exhaustion. These strategies fed into already damaged family relationships with both Terence and the children, who felt bereft of her support.

Conclusion

This exploration of teacher stress and family emotion shows that emotion in the family is a social and cultural phenomenon. Family systems became the holding environments for stress emotion from multiple sites, where workers, partners, children and elders each compete in the emotional labour market. For these teachers the familial sphere was not a refuge at this stage but a site of emotional trauma. Emotion from family and working spheres collided, increasing vulnerability to stress-related illness for both the teachers and their families. This is because the family produces its own stressors – coping with quadruple shifts, bereavement and illness, children's problems, clashes between work and home, possibly marital difficulties. There is spillover between home and work, one aggravating the other, stress worsening in the interplay. In the circumstances of the families of our teachers, they tip each other over the edge in a spiral of decline. Emotional climates and competences deteriorate, emotional labour increases and becomes unmanageable, causing health, relationships and identities to deteriorate.

However, just as the family is not only a blissful haven for recovery, it is not solely a site of trauma. As we shall see in chapter 4, the family did provide solace for some of our teachers at a later point in the stress career. Also, not all families show the same features as those discussed here. It is conceivable that with change or removal of one or more of those features (such as bereavements at key points, or having to care for elderly parents as well as children, home and holding down a job), the family might have assumed more of a therapeutic role from an earlier stage, possibly heading off the stress. By the same token, changes in one or more of the features at work might also have headed off the downward spiral.

3

The Downward Spiral: The Loss of Identity

So far, we have considered the origins of teacher stress. We now move to the effects of stress on the teachers, which we see primarily in terms of identity. Stress is a process in which the personal identity undergoes assault and battery, total anomie and ultimately transformation. Borrowing from the idea of status passage, we find three major phases (Van Gennep, 1960). In the first phase, there is the traumatic separation from the old identity and the structures and cultures that sustained it. Many cherished aspects of the self are attacked and become separated from the personal identity until the individual becomes completely disorientated. Secondly, there is transition, moving to the depths of despair where rock bottom is reached, but also the beginnings of redemption, which is encouraged by the stressed person experiencing 'cocooning', the influence of significant others and the gradual reassertion of the self. Thirdly, there is reincorporation in, or realignment with, society, when a sense of personal identity is recovered or reconstructed. In some ways, however, this is too neat a division. The identity passage is an unscheduled one (Glaser and Strauss, 1971). There are no historical or cultural norms to guide the teachers through. They have, on the whole, to find their own way, and doing so makes for a great deal of confusion during stress, and for uneven passages. But, we would argue, the underlying pattern of recovery takes this form.

The identity passage is navigated through the emotions. Extreme, profound, unsettling emotions are experienced at times of stress. There are clearly connections between the onset and nature of these emotions and the restructuring of education and schools that has dominated the last decade or so (Hargreaves, 1994; Troman and Woods, 2001). These emotions also have meaning at the micro level. Situating them within the identity passage enables us to see how they are shaped and changed by the course of the passage, driven by the need for individuals to re-engage with society. As Denzin (1984: 6) argues,

> All experiences of being emotional are situational, reflective and relational ...The self of the person stands in the centre of the emotions that are experienced. Self-feelings constitute the inner essence, or core of emotionality.

There is another angle to our discussion. Much debate rages about what is happening to identities in the current age. This is well represented in the work of Giddens, who draws a contrast between conceptions of post-modernity and 'radicalised modernity'. The former lays emphasis on the dislocating character of current social transformations; on the self as 'dissolved or dismembered by the fragmentation of experience'; on the powerlessness of individuals in the face of globalising tendencies; and on the 'emptying' of day-to-day life as the result of the intrusion of abstract systems. His own preferred 'radicalised modernity', by contrast, points to a more dialectical set of circumstances, whereby 'active processes of reflexive self-identity are made possible, where possibilities for both powerlessness and empowerment exist, and there is an active engagement with abstract systems, 'involving appropriation as well as loss' (Giddens, 1990: 150). Our research contributes to this debate.

Our view of identity is outlined elsewhere:

> We largely follow Snow and Anderson's (1987) construction, with some modifications, distinguishing among social identities, personal identities, and self-concept. Social identities are 'attributed or imputed to others in an attempt to place or situate them as social objects.' (p.1347) These are largely 'imputations based primarily on information gleaned on the basis of appearance, behaviour, and the location and time of the action'. In the context of our research, we find the notion of an 'assigned social identity' (Ball, 1972) useful.These are imputations based on desired or prescribed appearance etc. Personal identities refer to the 'meanings attributed to the self by the actor,' and are 'self-designations and self-attributions brought into play during the course

> of interaction' (*ibid.*). They may be consistent or inconsistent with social identities. The self-concept is the 'overarching view of oneself as a physical, social, spiritual, or moral being', and is 'a kind of working compromise between idealized images and imputed social identities' (p.1348). We shall be concerned with teachers' personal identities, which 'provide a glimpse of the consistency or inconsistency between social identities and self-concept' (*ibid.*). We make a further distinction between 'substantial' and 'situational' identities. Ball (1972) used these terms to distinguish between more enduring identities and more transient ones given meaning by their contextual location. (Woods and Jeffrey, 2002, pp.89-90).

During the 1970s and early 1980s, there seemed to be considerable consistency between social identity and self-concept among teachers (see, for example, Nias, 1989). But after the restructuring reforms of the late 1980s and 90s, identities have become less isomorphic as teachers have struggled with a new assigned social identity which has been at variance with their self-concept (Woods *et al*, 1997; Woods and Jeffrey, 2002). This struggle is epitomised in the careers of our teachers' stress, and is well illustrated, we feel, through the concept of identity passage.

In the next three chapters we examine the structure and process of the identity passage during a time of stress; explore how the extreme, negative emotions involved at all stages are socially structured; and consider how these matters bear on theoretical approaches to identity-construction during late modernity. The chapters are organised around the three stages of the identity passage.

The Road to Separation: assaults on the self

During the downward spiral of the stress career, the self becomes detached from society. The extremes of emotion illustrate the traumatic nature of this process, but these emotions are socially meaningful in that 1) they arise from the interaction between the social conditions in which these teachers live and work and the personal identities they had established for themselves prior to restructuring with its new social identity; 2) an identity change of some kind is necessary; there has to be a new resolution of self with the new social identity; 3) this process is going to be radical and painful – extreme negative emotions express this pain, but also have the effect of detaching the self from the old identity. In this sense, though traumatic, separation is the first stage towards reconstruction of personal identities.

We might characterise the key components of a well-founded personal identity as involving a measure of autonomy and control; a sense of balance and equilibrium; a holism and unification of component parts, what Giddens terms a 'coherent narrative'; a synchronism of personal and social spheres, of self and role. Giddens also speaks about ontological security – 'confidence in the continuity of personal identity' and 'a sense of continuity and order in events, including those not directly within the perceptual environment of the individual' (Giddens, 1991: 243). The identity is rewarding in a number of intrinsic ways and heightens self-esteem, confidence, emotional security, sense of well-being and trust. It enables us to relate to others in productive, convivial and predictable ways. To a large extent, identities are defined and gain their meaning through relationships with others. Gender is a powerful factor in identities. Identity is a reflexive process rather than an immutable state, and requires time and space for that reflection. At its core might be an 'essential', or an historical, self – values, beliefs, attitudes, proclivities, temperament – that the individual holds dear as 'the real me' and is loath to compromise.

All these key aspects of the teachers' personal identity came under attack, and became separated from the self. The overwhelming experience was one of loss.

Loss of emotional skills

Teachers lost key personal emotional competences vital to teaching tasks (Goleman, 2001). Teachers spoke of losing confidence in both the educational system and their own professionalism. 'The situation becomes so stressful you lose confidence in your own abilities. I had a real bashing in terms of self-esteem' (Maureen). For Andrew,

> ... [school management] took away every bit of confidence ... It wasn't just that they made me believe I was useless at teaching. I felt useless at living. If I tried to do something, I'd do it wrong, break it, make it worse, which is why I sat about doing nothing. I'd maintained the car before and I thought: 'I can't do it. I'll do it wrong, mess it up. Better get it done properly at the garage'.

Teachers also lost key social competences. Empathy with students, colleagues and families suffered. 'Good rapport with the kids diminished. A sense of antipathy developed between me and students' (Edward). 'I was under so much stress, I was not performing well, not my normal tactful self, criticising more than I should' (Margot). Listening skills were impaired:

> If you're stressed out and worried about being all 'bloused up' and what not, you get tight arsed. You can't hear what's happening. You're not child-centred any more because you become self-centred. (Charlotte)

Teachers lost the abilities to sense and understand others' feelings, and to provide opportunities for developing children's emotional skills:

> I lost sight of the big picture, worrying about the minutiae of the job ... Seeing kids at the end of the day with reports and chasing those up rather than getting down to why is this kid on report? What are we going to do to change his/her behaviour? (Ralph)

They could no longer provide students, colleagues, family and friends with support. Alicia, Terence's wife, felt he 'lost time to listen to what [she] was saying'. Edward 'wasn't sympathetic to [his] wife Olivia when she needed it, or as interested in what she was doing'. Gareth, a part-time pastor spent all his time

> ... marking, preparing lessons, thinking new schemes, new ways. Almost total attention directed towards [teaching] part-time. As a result, the pastoring wasn't what folks needed .... I'd totally thrown away any work God had for me.

Teachers were no longer able to provide emotional services for others:

> When I didn't go into work and encourage other people to smile, I thought you're in a bad state if you can't smile, and you're in an even worse state if you can't encourage other people to smile. I couldn't cheer myself up, let alone cheer anyone else up. (Maureen, nicknamed Smiler)

The stress label was shaming. 'To admit you're suffering from stress is classed as a shame on you' (Margot). 'It's not socially acceptable to have any sort of mental illness' (Celia). Andrew felt 'mortified' and 'humiliated' at being called to account in front of the school governing body. Similarly, Emily felt 'thoroughly humiliated, professionally let down'. Such degradation ceremonies (Garfinkel, 1956) were the symbol of a new order and authority, conveying meaning not only to the individuals concerned but also to others. Typically, those involved felt ashamed of 'letting down both others' and their own ideals, their standards' (Maureen). For Giddens (1991: 65), shame bears 'directly on self-identity because it is essentially anxiety about the adequacy of the narrative by means of which the individual sustains a coherent biography'. It was made worse by stigmatisation (Goffman, 1964). 'Having problems with employment [is] a social taboo' (Celia). Alex felt that 'everybody's looking at me. There's no doubt people's perception changed completely.' Teachers feared the stress label would be permanently associated with their having reduced levels of competence, and would cast a long-lasting blemish on their careers, irrevocably staining their reputations:

> If stress were on my record, the chances of me getting out would disappear. I wanted a clean bill of health. My doctor wanted me to take tranquillizers. I utterly refused. He asked me to see a counsellor. I had one meeting. He couldn't do anything for me because I was so anti-counselling. I was 100 per cent determined I wasn't going through anything that someone could say: 'Oh. She's had to take tranquillizers, had to have counselling because she couldn't cope'. I didn't want it written in my notes, didn't want anyone thinking I couldn't hold down another job. I was absolutely paranoid about it, didn't want anything to put a fly in the ointment. (Jessica)

Celia's Head 'wouldn't write [her] a reference. I was only there a term officially, only taught six weeks. He said he didn't feel he knew me well enough. I suppose that's fair, but it's still a bit of a blot on that time'. Charlotte felt 'Nobody will want someone who's been off with stress. I feel so depressed. What a bloody waste it is! All those years, all that training.' Early detection, diagnosis and therapeutic action were hindered through withholding information from doctors, 'not being prepared to admit it was stress-related' (Ralph). 'I pulled the wool over my doctor's eyes' (Celia). The emotional labour involved in concealing negative feelings and managing the self exacerbated exhaustion. Stress was thus viewed not as a feature of modern life but as individual weakness, a sign of vulnerability, associated with incompetence. Concealment caused a reduction in seeking help, an increase in energy expenditure, and it reduced emotional awareness and perceived levels of competence.

Loss of emotion regulation

Teachers experienced 'emotional dysregulation' – losses in their ability to control, regulate, and recover from emotional states (Gottman *et al*, 1997). They experienced problems with their 'ability to manage frustration, anger, anxiety and sadness, avoiding self-destructive behaviour, and monitoring self-criticism' (Klein, 1997). When you are stressed, 'things go out of balance' (Sally), 'like the swing of a thermostat ... a bit too hot, then too cold, then too hot again' (Andrew). Teachers experienced much emotional turbulence. They felt they were caught in a 'downward spiral' (Edward), in a 'whirlpool of distress' (Terence), 'trapped on a treadmill' (Stephen), in the 'depths of despair' (Charlotte). Feeling 'out of control' of both selves and situations was a major factor:

> Somewhere along the way I lost control, almost as though I needed to let off steam. It came out in quite a lot of loopy ways ... I don't think I lived in the real world any of the time. (Morag)

Rachel 'kept bursting into tears'. Charlotte was 'crying a lot but didn't know why, over things I wouldn't normally cry about'. Edward could not overcome his frustration and disappointment with students who did not want to learn. The teachers felt very strongly about unresolved issues in their school. Sally felt 'absolute fury ... I was absolutely livid'. She recalled 'going mad' at her deputy head, 'berserck. I was trying to shut up, but it all came out'. Maureen was 'screaming inside'. They became less and less capable of avoiding self-destructive behaviours. They lost their tempers – Marcus, for example, experiencing a 'red mist' of 'uncontrollable explosive emotion' and 'verbal aggression' to his pupils. He described 'going over the top':

> I'd fly off the handle very quickly, yell and swear at them from a very short distance, get my face right up against theirs, tell them what I thought about them, how they should be behaving. Bullying really. It would make my stomach churn inside. I'd feel physically clammy or hot, shaking. Because I was yelling and bawling, my eyes would water.

> My vision, my voice would go. I'd actually hurt my throat. I must have been in a high emotional state to react like that.

Ralph recalled 'one or two judgement calls' where he 'behaved unprofessionally, verbally abusing kids', which left him feeling 'disgusted, my standards totally compromised'. Charlotte recollected standing in front of her headteacher, eyes tight shut, fists clenched, screaming, 'I hate you! I hate you! I hate you!' 'Losing your temper is a sign you're not a 'good' teacher' (Celia). Morag

> ... got wilder and wilder. It was like a massive explosion! I exploded because, as well as not having input from the bottom end up, there was nobody to put a cap on it. There was only me. There was nobody saying 'Stop'. Nobody to control me, and I couldn't control myself. I just got swept away.

A sense of autonomy is essential to emotional well-being, concerning, as it does, 'subjective perceptions of who controls the work process, and the extent of identity involvement in it' (Bulan *et al*, 1997: 239). The teachers felt they could not influence change processes, Ralph feeling like a 'puppet, with somebody else pulling the strings'. As she experienced day-to-day control 'being taken away', Maureen became 'a very unhappy person. It was creating anxiety and a great sense of guilt'.

Margot suffered one of the characteristic 'guilt traps' of teaching (Hargreaves, 1994: 142). She was

> ... full of guilt ... Getting over the guilt, being away from school, was absolutely horrendous. I'd let my students down ... I'd let my family down, let my mother down. She's been dead for years, but I felt this incredible guilt thing.

The 'trap' is the pressure of the job, which had caused her absence in the first place, and which then induced guilt in a teacher who, typically, was strongly influenced by the work ethic – which then caused more stress. Similarly, Stephen felt 'guilty about what was not going right, not being on top of the job. I wasn't delivering the quality of education I'd been used to and that I wanted to do. That spirals back, fuels the failing part of it'.

Teachers experienced meta-emotions, 'feelings about feelings' (Gottman *et al*, 1997: 6), characterised by recursiveness, 'acting back on themselves in never-ending loops' (Scheff, 1990: 18). Teachers described feeling ashamed of feeling ashamed, angry about feeling angry, ashamed at feeling anger, angry at feeling shame, ashamed at feeling jealous. 'My fear of failure was controlling me' (Andrew). Jonathon 'felt shame at being angry'. Alex described his fear of anticipated social transactions with students and colleagues as a 'nightmare':

> The fear of going to school, going out of the house, it was hard getting there. I remember driving, screaming in tears, saying: 'You have got to go. You have got to go'. Fighting literally. Frightened to get back ... I didn't fear when I was there. It was going. It was fear of fear.

Teachers and their families recounted how ruminating anger heightened already high emotional states. Teachers held destructive conversations with themselves. 'I've always spoken to myself internally. When I was young it was very positive thinking. Not any more' (Alex). Fiona described the atmosphere at home as 'scary', as her father's rumination intensified. 'You always knew there was something wrong because everywhere you'd go, all you could hear was this mumble, mumble, mumble'.

Heightened emotional states reduced the teachers' emotional capital so severely that emotional turbulence from the past resurfaced. Charlotte was 'crying so much because of all the baggage I'd got, crying for myself as well as for what happened to anyone else. I was thinking: 'Yes, *my* injustices, *my* injustices''. Sally felt her 'subconscious' affecting her 'consciously, repression. There's a lot of stuff there that's probably very disturbed. It goes beyond Mr Ballantyne and that damned school. Everything – like that merger'. Celia too viewed her breakdown as 'a throwback to a year of repressed feelings. ... I felt so angry! I'd repressed a lot of things about being controlled. It had to come out in the end'. For Alex a combination of repressed grief and feelings of failure 'all came flooding back'.

Childhood emotion re-surfaced for Luke, Jonathon, Emily, Rachel, Rebecca and Marcus. They experienced 'flashbacks' from past emotional traumas. 'The maggots are still there', said Marcus. For Emily, 'years of chronic abuse and trauma' from her two troubled marriages and her school experiences triggered memories of childhood hospitalisation, separation anxiety, abandonment and depression. Rebecca's experience of sexual assault

> ... got in touch with other things. It triggered in me strange thoughts and feelings. I feared it had taken the lid off something, that if anything happened again, I might not keep control .... I feared my own reactions very much.

Jonathon's decision to put his mother in a residential home 'brings on a lot of past life experiences that you really want to be pushed away, start coming back to you'.

Marcus explained his strategy of putting accumulated experiences in

> ... the bottom drawer ... The divorce was the big one. I didn't deal with it. ... You suppress it for a long, long time. Then something else comes in, and you stick that in. Then somebody dies. You put that in. You have a big argument, or fall out with somebody, and you put that in. Eventually your bottom drawer emotionally gets full, and the next thing overflows. That's when your problems start. It's the reliving of the emotion that would make me cry or make me angry.

Luke used the same metaphor:

> The drawer was certainly getting full, with all that unease and unrest at school, feeling unsettled in school, the environment I was in at home, and with not grieving properly for the end of the relationship. Not knowing where I was going. That's when it all started to get bad.

Energies spent coping with emotional turbulence during the lengthy downward spiral reduced their capacity for managing current emotion, recovering from emotional distress and building emotional capital (Williams, 1998). Rebecca felt 'very vulnerable, very fragile ... The effort of wondering what would come out next'. Teachers lost their motivation. Alex 'didn't have the energy, time or emotional strength'. Unable to deal with these emotions, understand them or prevent their escalation in social encounters, the teachers became caught in 'feeling traps', where brief, primary emotion states are converted into long-term secondary states, even more impervious to normalisation (Scheff, 1990: 171), and where 'our integrity and our selves have been placed in question' (Hargreaves, 1998a: 840).

In addition, emotional dysregulation undermined their gendered identities. Both men and women perceived themselves as breaking fundamental cultural 'laws' (Scheff, 1990). Stress was experienced as one of the many ways a man could 'lose face' (Edward) and consequently power and status (Kemper, 1978). As Alex explained, 'the job defines a man'. 'Stress is seen wrongly as almost a defeat to one's masculinity' (Ralph). The stress experience proved an emasculating experience as feelings of loss of control were magnified through the expression of painful emotion, seen as incompatible with certain masculinities (Doyle, 1989). Because Stephen could not speak with colleagues or family about his distress, he felt 'the more things started to go wrong, the less I'm prepared to talk about it, the feelings of failure. I don't want to expose the failing too much ... everything just seemed to add to this sense of failure'. Andrew 'wouldn't have thought [stress] would affect me ... It's not masculine to have emotions, feelings and things ... Big boys don't cry'. Their failure to live up to what they perceived as the 'proper' male role added to the men's sense of shame.

Women teachers also felt they had failed to live up to their gendered identity. Charlotte believed that working class women should be 'strong ... It's cissy to cry, even more so for a girl around here. You have to be even stronger ... If you're a woman in secondary, you must have balls'. Margot felt shame at failing to live up to the female role she perceived as hers, derived from her northern cultural identity. Women earned their keep and were proud to do so. However, Margot 'felt that I'd let so many people down and I'd never catch up ... This is taboo to my lifestyle, totally taboo.'

For the women, nurturing others was a core component of their identity. The 'motherhood mandate' continues to provide a powerful social expectation within gendered social roles (Russo, 1976). As school pressures increased, their identity became threatened by feelings of shame surrounding the 'bad mother'. Margot said she was

> ... being the most awful mother. I'd given up a whole year of my life for school. I hadn't once, during the times I'd lain awake all night, ever thought of my own children. Not once! I'd only thought of other people's children.

Loss of positive emotional experiences

> I like the positive stress side of this job, but you can't deal with that when there are negative stresses of that magnitude. (Alex)

The teachers' lives had previously been filled with rewarding emotional relationships with their students and colleagues, 'sitting talking to kids in lessons, teasing things out of them, seeing the proverbial light bulb light up. Kids can be a real problem but also the creation of job satisfaction' (Ralph). Similarly, Maureen

> ... really enjoyed it. In principle it's the most wonderful thing in the world to walk into a classroom, give something of your own particular knowledge, open up students' minds to all those wonderful things in the world that are waiting for them – like being in charge of a wonderful Christmas box of goodies every child can have.

By this stage, however, teaching no longer provided the positive emotional experiences with students that it used to within a more child-centred discourse (Nias, 1989). Charlotte 'used to love that feeling that you'd got a buzz in the room. It would feed you. It was like a charge. Like group lift. Kids do it so easily. That energy, that spirituality, that life force, is definitely lacking. I'm not being fed'. Previously, Margot had always 'loved' her work. 'In those days it was a vocation, something you thoroughly enjoyed'. Jonathon felt 'a lot of fun [had] gone out of the job ... Where do I get my highs? To be honest, not many places'.

Positive emotional experiences with colleagues dwindled. Some would argue that interdependence is the most productive state of such relationships (Little, 1990). Support networks disappeared under the pressures of work, which was doubly unfortunate since collegial support has an important role in ameliorating stress (Punch and Tuettemann, 1996). Gareth found 'very little common ground, very little camaraderie' in his department, which contributed to his 'feeling isolated'. Intensification had spread into all areas. 'You don't have time to socialise with colleagues. It's a professionally busy world, a lot of women too busy to speak at work' (Rebecca). 'We used to have cream cakes at birthdays' (Stephen).

> It got to the stage where every time we did socialise all people were doing was moaning about the job. Teachers will talk of nothing else, especially when they're very depressed. Over the last five or six years it's just got worse. (Margot)

Teaching is a creative art (Woods, 1996b), and among our teachers were some highly creative individuals. Under the experience of stress, however, the creative self was lost. Luke was 'obsessed with music. It's my life', but he found less and less time and motivation for composition and extemporisation. Morag, who taught art, 'used to think: 'Hey, teaching, it's brilliant. I'm doing my hobby for a job'. Then I realised I wasn't doing my hobby for a hobby'. Margot, too, ceased her own artistic endeavours. Rebecca, another artist,

> hung on to [her painting] through all sorts of traumas ... as an escape route when things have been hard. I couldn't throughout the whole of last year, just lost it completely. It's like losing my soul, very much part of my identity.

Loss of the creative self not only impinged on personal identity, it negatively affected teaching:

> Because I was stressed, my creative ability was not functioning, my ability to think of new ways. I certainly wasn't applying any of my own educational communicative teaching. I wasn't able to think about the method at all. (Rachel)

There was less time generally for enjoying positive emotional experiences or health promoting activities. 'Hobbies that should make me relax didn't; got me more stressed out, always going wrong' (Rachel).

> It's very important, having a stressful job, to have a social life and family life to keep the balance. My social life went totally to pot ... I was working every night, weekends, marking, work piling up and piling up, everything totally work-oriented. I was struggling, not keeping up with my social life, which I really had enjoyed. (Rebecca)

Important therapeutic outlets were lost. William ceased tending his allotment. Luke 'stopped reading ... I couldn't do my music, run a relationship, and do my job at the same time ...'. Margot 'hadn't time' for 'church, to meditate and pray. I do a lot of writing. For a year I hadn't. When I analysed what I'd done, everything had gone for school, a whole year of my life for school, appalling'. Edward stopped playing tennis – 'too busy ... I used to be very fond of singing. My singing voice is gone'. Andrew, a keen photographer,

> ... lost interest, stopped going to photographic club, stopped learning Italian, couldn't be bothered to go out. Things I enjoy doing, I didn't want to do. Struggling through the day, looking over my shoulder all the time, get home with a sigh of relief, collapsing into the chair, then the next day the same.

The self, as a reflexive self, needs time and space for reflexivity (Hargreaves, 1994). However, intensification had eaten into not only what were previously recuperatory and self-reinforcing 'back regions' of school (Goffman, 1959), but home life also. There was a relentless, lengthy, wearing down process, with no time for recovery. The school holidays, once used to 'recuperate, achieve a better balance, overcome the stress of the year' (Marcus), were now occupied with work, re-writing syllabi and adapting to new subject areas:

> If you don't recuperate you've a problem. By the time October comes round, you're at an even lower ebb. I'd never relaxed in the summer. Went back under par. Stress and strains occurred straight away, heavier timetable, more aggro from management, a little bit of management bullying, then came down with flu. (Marcus)

As unfavourable conditions prevailed, opportunities for safeguarding and building emotional capital (Williams, 1998) ceased. Teachers experienced a 'gradual deterioration in the quality of life' (Marcus), a catalogue of 'big disappointments' (Edward), 'a year of great tension gradually wore me down' (Andrew), pressures 'building up over a long period of time' (Stephen). Negative affect increased. 'I was very negative about it all' (Terence). 'I'd be unreasonably hurt, like having PMT all the time. Anything they said that was a bit out, I'd get very upset by it' (Charlotte). Margot, situating her distress within general world developments, was

> ... so sick of the world. The twentieth century was terrifying, the fast pace of life, people using me, and abusing me. It wasn't just one. It was hundreds! I felt everybody was doing that. You tend to start looking into things with almost an evil eye.

Jessica's husband Frank, related how

> ... the stress and mental anguish was just totally getting on top of her. If you'd talked to Jessica a few months ago, she would have said there were none [positive experiences]. Everything's negative, nothing's positive.

Loss of physical health

> I was obviously very stressed, not sleeping. I became depressed. At the time I didn't notice it – a whole spiralling downwards. My sense of humour went. Physically and mentally I was ill. The whole thing snowballed. One thing led to another. My blood pressure went through the roof, my diabetes, my blood sugar level, shooting all over the place. (Terence)

Emotional states engendered physical illness, and vice versa: 'chemical signals create and/or organise behavioural states ... their activity and regulatory feedback loops play important roles in initiating and sustaining the mood and emotional states that can promote disease' (Leventhal and Patrick-Miller, 1993: 373). Possible health consequences of the long-term effects of stress caused these teachers further anxiety, sustaining feedback loops:

> I'd become dependent on the adrenaline I must have been living on to sustain that workload. Somewhere down the road I'll end up paying the price for stress, permanent long-term damage to major organs. (Ralph)

Somatisation, where people are aware of the physical sensations accompanying emotional experiences but not of the emotions themselves, but cannot accurately interpret their bodily experiences (Steiner, 2000), was a common response by these teachers to stress. They reported exhaustion, psychosomatic disorders, deficient immune systems, disorders in sleep patterns, nightmares, all reacting upon each other. Physical illnesses came because

> ... you've become exhausted. My head feels fuzzy, as if in cotton wool, as if the room is slightly darkened, a fog around me. My lateral vision is impaired. I can only see straight in front. I want to go back to sleep, my body, my brain, saying no. (Marcus)

Teachers in the study reported a range of psychosomatic disorders. Emily viewed her spinal pain as 'emotional pain ... a vicious circle of tension'. Similarly, Rachel's

> ... body was shouting. When you're stressed, you can't breathe properly. You end up with physical symptoms building up, backache, aches and pains, problems with my neck. As I got more and more tense, everything was going wrong, pains moving around the body, went on for months, the tic in my eye, eyes hurting.

Evidence suggests that existing medical conditions are exacerbated by stress (Lazarus and Lazarus, 1994). Taking time off work to manage personal illness precipitated feelings of guilt. Terence, for example, was

> ... made to feel very guilty when I went to the diabetic clinic ... There was no flexibility. You were there when school started. You had to be there at the end. There was no way of getting out during the day if you needed to. Heaven forbid if I needed to go to the dentist!

Symptoms were manifest within differing sites in accordance with individual emotional, physical and cognitive vulnerability (Bartlett, 1998). Rebecca, for instance, had recurrent gum infections. Marcus and Ralph developed adult asthma. Stomach problems and chest pains were common. For Margot, chronic anxiety led to dislocation of the jaw:

> The pain was incredible, like neuralgia all the time, headaches right across the whole of my skull to the point where I couldn't bear it. I couldn't sleep. I thought I was having terrible teeth problems. I had root canal fillings done and taken out, teeth taken out.

Celia, Charlotte, Emily, Maureen and Rachel all felt that 'women's troubles' were a common 'masking element' (Celia), directing attention away from an early diagnosis of stress. For example, Celia and her GP interpreted the changes in her bodily experiences as being due to hormonal imbalance: 'I thought it was just PMT, the anxiety, the fluid retention. I was very irritable for several months'. Her doctor prescribed 'Prozac, two weeks before my period'. Celia, like other women in this sample, tried 'alternative therapies, the well woman clinic, evening primrose oil. I was just in the midst of trying all of these different therapies when I broke down and had to sign off for six weeks. It was obvious that this was a forerunner of depression'. Charlotte experienced her anaemia as a physical symptom of emotional trauma in the workplace:

> The place [was] draining my life's blood, heavy periods, constant periods, because I was stressed. I reckon they were taking my life's blood and it was happening to me physically. Once I stopped [work] it stopped happening physically. Because I'm not losing so much, I've got all my iron back. I haven't got those dark rings under my eyes.

A vicious, reinforcing cycle of chronic fatigue developed, as anxiety, retrospective and prospective, led to early waking. An inability to turn off intrusive thoughts and feelings increased emotional exhaustion. For some, a pattern emerged: working late into the night, often not going to bed until two or three in the morning, and rising early. Many suffered sleep deprivation. Three hours sleep became the norm for Ralph and Alex, Ralph and Charlotte all experienced nights when they didn't sleep at all. Dreams were disturbing, and were interpreted as signals to the self, signs to 'slow down. Take your time' (Charlotte).

> Kids kept falling in fucking wells. I lost fifteen. I was falling down, crashing through trees, undergrowth, or wells, trying to hang on, slipping down, down, down, and I thought 'I'm breaking down here'. (Charlotte)

Some also lost their cognitive agility. As Goleman (1995: 149) writes, when people are emotionally upset, they 'cannot remember, attend, learn, or make decisions clearly. As one management consultant put it 'stress makes people stupid''. The teachers experienced losses in information processing, memory and decision-making, linked to feelings of exhaustion, confidence, anxiety and competence. 'Once in a stressful situation, you can't think. It all goes blank' (Rachel). 'My thought processes were showing signs of stress. We always mention the physical side but I wasn't thinking clearly' (Ralph). 'My brain wasn't working properly' (Maureen). 'I was losing my memory' (Sally). Stress made for more errors and 'worry about mistakes knocked my confidence further' (Andrew). Stress also impaired the ability to multi-task and to deal with computers, which are key teacher competences.

These socially engendered physical states all contributed to the sense of anomic disorder, of losing touch with reality, of being beyond the social pale.

Emotional estrangement

In the absence of effective organisational strategies, the teachers turned to emotion-focused options to reduce the impact of emotional distress on their daily life. According to Freudenberger and Richelson (1980: 104), individuals experiencing burnout, 'governed by the work ethic ... unwittingly select a cure ... which intensifies the burnout, spreading it faster and further'. While efficacious temporarily, the adoption of emotion-focused measures only accelerated decline in the long run. They did not get to grips with the basic problem – the assault on the personal identity and the need to re-engage.

All interviewees used commonly ascribed stress management techniques. Maureen, for example, who was proactive about stress reduction, explored relaxation techniques, diet, boosting the immune system, vitamins, monitoring cholesterol levels, yoga, meditation and breathing exercises. She found these strategies helpful at first. Finding directed time for exercise was an added stressor, so she walked to school. Visualisation exercises reduced stressful social transactions:

> I took my mind off for a fleeting second. That brought me into a calm state again. I got exceptionally good at that. I had my pebble, like the Eskimo worry stone. I visualised my pebble in any situation I felt I couldn't control.

Anticipatory cognitive strategies helped her combat negative thinking:

> It was very difficult to stop thinking ahead in negative ways. I tried to redress the balance, visualising the worse thing that could happen about things I was frightened of, and form a strategy for how I was going to cope.

But with the continued mismatch between resources and situational demands, personal stress management techniques proved ineffective in the long term for these teachers. Stephen for instance, 'knew procedures to cope with stress – relaxation tapes, meditation, exercise. I found I wasn't able to do that, and do the job as well. The two wouldn't sit well together'.

Palliative strategies gave immediate relief to disturbing bodily experiences, temporarily easing the pain. Margot and Charlotte resumed their dependence on nicotine. Alcohol dependence was widespread, giving rise to other symptoms such as disturbed sleep patterns. Self-medication was common. In the case of Ralph, Emily and William, painkillers for repeated headaches/migraine led to dependency on 'paracetamol' (Ralph), 'aspirin, in my briefcase, in the car' (William), and Emily 'took travel sickness pills first so I didn't throw up the painkillers. If you want to keep going, it's not easy, because you get a bit stupid with travel sickness pills. You can't drive'. Margot, Maureen, Celia, Alex, Luke and Emily explored alternative therapies such as evening primrose oil, aromatherapy and homeopathy. Charlotte turned to the coping mechanism she used in her youth, amphetamines, to help 'control feelings':

> I wasn't getting support when I needed it most. I felt I was losing my mind. It took me back twenty years. I thought: 'What the hell are you doing?' I'd have lost my job if I'd carried on. That was scary.

The teachers also managed emotion by means of defence mechanisms, a common strategy when problems are seen to be outside personal control (Folkman, 1997). Denial was uppermost. 'Something like stress, you shelve it under the carpet' (Charlotte).

> Stressed? Me? I'm not stressed. You go into denial straight away. One of the biggest failings individuals make – they try and convince themselves they're not suffering stress. I shrugged it off. Whatever happens I can cope. (Ralph)

Displacement was common. Luke's negative emotion, for example, emerged in music:

> The year I was trying to mend, my release wasn't a good release. I was out performing in the week, till 2/3 o'clock in the morning, getting up and going to work at seven. It's just a cacophony, a big angry noise. It was all very just on the edge, so much negativeness, hostility, so self-destructive. I couldn't carry on like that.

Teachers distanced themselves from others – Andrew could not 'let anyone help. It was *my* problem'. Margot removed herself from the teaching world as much as possible, spending her lunch break in town, for example. She avoided all contact with teaching and teachers outside school:

> It's this fear, this intrusion on my life. It's something I have to keep separate to keep sane. I wouldn't ever talk about teaching so there's no staff involved in my life. I won't have anybody from school here. If I go to a car boot sale and see a member of staff, my stomach sinks. I feel sick.

Their defence mechanisms reflected ongoing social transactions and the affective requirements of the teaching experience, the 'organisationally imposed rules requiring specific facial and bodily displays' that prescribe occupationally relevant behaviour (Bulan *et al*, 1997: 237). Teachers reported how their emotion management was dictated by direct and indirect managerial supervision and growing external controls over their working lives. Jonathon spoke of

> ... people's expectations of me. They expect me to work hard. They expect me to smile all the time, to run around doing jobs, to introduce new initiatives, to get involved with this, that, the other, to say: 'Yes' to anyone.

Celia

> ... wasn't feeling I could be me. I was trying to be me in the classroom, but it wasn't popular with management. The sort of teacher that's wanted – someone who toes the party line, I've never fitted that mould, always been a bit of a maverick, too individual, a free spirit. I tried hard but that's very emotionally draining.

Teachers donned an emotional mask to hide their true feelings. 'Terence's quite good at putting a mask on. He just shut off' (Alicia). Andrew 'didn't enjoy teaching', and

> ... put on as vague a face as possible. In school I was as miserable as sin, still trying to make silly jokes, smile. Particular girls saw through me: 'What's the matter, Sir? There's something wrong!'

Such behaviour heightened feelings of inauthenticity. 'I wasn't being true to myself' (Luke). Maureen 'was being made to go through the *motions* of a 'good' teacher but I didn't *feel* a good teacher any more'. Such 'deep acting' puts people at risk of 'losing the signal function of feeling' (Hochschild, 1983: 21). Communication with the emotional self was profoundly damaged; Luke, for example, shunned

> ... down times where I wasn't doing anything, just sit there doing nothing. I wasn't comfortable to just sit there by myself, because, when I sat there myself, suddenly: Whooo! I realised it was just a big front I was living through.

Edward filled his time 'with routine, to avoid having to feel about it'. Much emotional energy was spent repressing emotion. Andrew 'bottled it up for so long'. Emotional labour was 'draining energy a lot, so you hadn't got the energy to rejuvenate yourself to keep going, and in teaching you do need to rejuvenate' (William).

Increasing numbers of teachers use prescribed medication to survive the stress of everyday life. Around one in ten primary headteachers reportedly take tranquillisers or anti-depressants (Passmore, 1997). Betablockers and tranquillisers/anti-depressants were prescribed to manage 'anxiety', 'stress-related reactive depression' and 'neurasthenia'. Maureen employed 'non-invasive, non-medication ways to keep blood pressure within bounds. For a while they could. I coped quite well. But as life got more tricky, it wasn't enough. I started on tablets, and the tablets didn't work'. 'They alleviated confrontations, made me more laid back' (Emily).

Using tranquillisers, however, added to emotional estrangement because they reduced the feeling of being in control. Rebecca felt

> ... everything was woozy, clouded, like tunnel vision ... I didn't recognise any of the feelings. It was masking, dulled all my senses down, hearing, feeling. I was barely operating, very artificial Mogadon levels, terrible ... I'd rather be in control and it hurting a bit. That's vital to me.

The drugs distanced teachers from students and colleagues, making them 'more detached, less emotionally involved, more laid back, less whizzy, more inclined to let things ride' (Celia). There were 'terrible side-effects, hangovers, half the next day wiped out' (Jonathon). Alex 'couldn't function, chemically I was just out with it'. Charlotte had difficulty staying awake. 'I call them dopey-athis tablets 'cos that's what they make me!' Teachers felt medication did little to control or cure their symptoms. Rebecca's panic attacks for example, 'continued. It didn't stop the dreams and the re-enactments'.

As reported by Cooperstock (1976), tranquillisers enabled individuals to maintain difficult or intolerable roles without dealing with the underlying causes, facilitating their return to work, sometimes against their doctors' advice. This was 'hard work. I felt slow in the mornings, the sedative effect. Needed to get up earlier, have coffee. I was OK to drive because I wasn't taking a very large dosage but nevertheless I had to be aware I was on it' (Celia). Rebecca found work 'very much more difficult ... numbed, in incredibly slow motion'. Celia 'had to rush around to do one and a half people's job. It did make me able to do the job better. I could fit more in, but it wasn't good for me'.

Teachers' resistance to, and unhappiness with, the social conditions of their teaching worlds was pathologised, medication locking them into problematic situations by its 'chemical curtain' (Hansen, 1989: 166), 'a physical way of making you not affected by the outside world' (Charlotte). It 'masked' the nature of the stressors, and gave an illusion of coping. Celia for example, found

> ... Prozac no good at all, too much of a high. I was even more anxious than before, pretty manic, rushing around. It was masking the fact that I was still gradually crumbling inside. I couldn't see it. Getting tireder and tireder. I thought I was coping well but I was too fast, too energetic, too anxious, cramming a lot of activities into each day, rushing around manically and feeling incompetent ... until it all fell to pieces, and I just had to stop. My poor little self couldn't cope any more!

Most of our teachers used such coping strategies for long periods, during which the nature of their distress was disguised. 'No-one knew I'd got a problem. I hid it well, an immaculate concealment. There was no way anybody seemed to recognise it' (Luke).

Withdrawing into a protective emotional shell can be a natural response to trauma, shielding us from further suffering. However, when attacks on identity are prolonged and trauma persists, emotional numbing becomes chronic. Emotional systems shut down, preventing the experience of pleasure as well as pain. Jonathon's 'lows follow the highs, so you can't always afford yourself the highs'. Edward put his mind

> ... as much as possible into neutral, not letting highs and lows impinge, trying to avoid the lows by cutting out the highs, switching off the emotions, a sort of detachment, as a defence mechanism, because if you did let the things that happen in school get to you, either the highs or the lows, then it would have painful repercussions. If you experience the highs then you've got to experience the lows as well and they both hurt too much. I gradually became more and more disaffected from everything to do with school.

Losing touch with their feelings, our teachers became powerless to understand their own and others' feelings, the effects, the strengths and limitations feelings provide, and their value in guiding decision-making. As Hochschild (1983: 29) points out, 'emotion, like seeing or hearing, is a way of knowing about the world'. Our teachers lost that way of knowing, with damaging consequences. With no legitimate emotionally literate outlet for their emotional pain, they froze up emotionally to protect themselves, commonly described as being in a 'fog'. They lost touch with their real feelings and their ability to 'be themselves'. William felt

> ... like a ship. The engine's broken down, steering's gone, drifting around, not knowing what direction I was going in, not focusing on any problems I was having. It deadens your sensitivity.

According to Goleman (2001), such emotional self-awareness is the foundation for all other emotional competences. 'I really haven't thought about myself, how I feel' (Andrew). Gareth 'wasn't aware of an inner rage. I'd come home angry. Couldn't say where I was directing my anger'. Margot 'hadn't thought about myself for a year; what's happening in my body, what's happening in my mind'. They lost their ability to self-monitor, with consequent limitations on secondary appraisal and re-appraisal. 'I'd got to sort through what had to be sorted, be in touch with it. I felt very out of touch with it' (Rebecca).

> I didn't realise I was suffering stress, put it down to problems with hearing ... I was knotted. The war around me prevented me seeing the knots. I didn't realise I was getting into trouble. (William)

'Now I know I've been really ill, how close I came to really burning out, going wacko' (Charlotte).

Loss of the essential self

Under such pressures, the teachers lost the sense of who they were. 'I didn't feel like myself at all. I couldn't recognise myself' (Rebecca). 'I couldn't believe that I was the person I was' (Andrew). 'You lose yourself when things are going badly. I lost myself for seven months' (Marcus). 'I wasn't me. The personality just gets wiped out, the person you think of as you' (Maureen). As Morag said, 'The stress of teaching splits you up so you don't know who you are any more'.

> I felt I'd completely failed as a teacher. Emotionally I find that very difficult because I see myself as a secondary teacher. That's what my persona is. I had a lot of emotional investment in it. (Celia)

The experience of stress revealed the presence of multiple 'mini-selves' and the emergence of 'shadow selves' (alter egos) (Abrams and Zweig, 1991), parts of selves that were feared and disliked, 'all the bad bits poking through because of stress... a very nasty side to me' (Sally). Luke 'was frightened of being eccentric, angry, rambling and ranting, abstract thoughts, revolutionary ideas'. He discovered 'large parts of [himself he] didn't like', their emergence 'a demonstration of me being out of control'. Phrases such as 'that's not me', 'that's not him/her', 'changed personality' were common. Margot became 'paranoiac', Ralph a 'monomaniac', Charlotte 'a very spoiled child'. Marcus' wife Pauline recalled him becoming 'enraged, not able to control his temper, wanting to throw these kids out of the windows, smash their faces in. This sort of violence is not like him at all'.

Ontological security no longer existed. We have seen how, prior to restructuring, teachers enjoyed high ontological security and a comparatively stable identity. Furthermore, this identity was holistic, with strong emotional association and no distinction between personal and professional roles (Nias, 1989). Teacher selves and personal selves were closely intertwined, bound up with vocational commitment, incurring large amounts of emotional investment. 'It was a vocation rather than a job. I don't want to lose my vocation in life ... losing all the tools, all the ways of doing, and it is a breaking down' (Charlotte). 'It used to be vocation. Now it's just a job' (Ralph). But restructuring has challenged the taken-for-grantedness of everyday life, the 'high level of reliability of the contexts of day-to-day social interaction' (Giddens, 1991: 36). Our teachers had lost their professional identities.

Marris (1993: 149) draws an analogy between loss and bereavement, asserting that 'any serious bereavement impairs the ability to attach meaning to events, and hence to learn from them how to survive'. Through the experience of stress, these teachers lost their ability to attach meaning to daily events and experiences, which in turn impaired their ability to come to terms with their losses, to incorporate change, and to move forward. Organisational factors reduced their 'transformative capacity' (Giddens, 1984), their ability to intervene in influencing the course of events. Our teachers became professionally, emotionally and cognitively de-skilled.

While recourse to emotion-focused strategies temporarily mitigated the effects of stress, they proved maladaptive in the long term, heightening burnout, hindering the early identification of stress, and hastening the descent through the downward spiral. Avoidance coping became entrenched, leading to coping failure. Coping failure was thus linked to job involvement and reduced levels of awareness, autonomy and control. As Siedman and Zager (1991: 213) conclude, 'without gaining a sense of control over their jobs, schoolteachers seem doomed to a devastating plethora of physical, psychological and social problems which will only worsen their teaching situations (creating a 'vicious circle')'.

If our research had ceased at this point, we might have been tempted to argue that our evidence supported postmodernistic interpretations that lay emphasis on dislocation, fragmentation, and the powerlessness of individuals before global forces. But we are only halfway through the stress career, and so far we have seen only the downward half. In chapter 4, we consider the second, transitional phase.

4

Transition: the Experience of Liminality

Victor Turner (1979) describes liminality as

> The state and process of mid-transition in a rite of passage. During the liminal period, the characteristics of the liminars are ambiguous, for they pass through a cultural realm that has few or none of the attributes of the past or coming state. Liminars are betwixt and between. The liminal state has frequently been likened to death; to being in the womb... (Turner, 1969, pp.94-96). Liminars are stripped of status and authority, removed from a social structure maintained and sanctioned by power and force, and levelled to a homogeneous social state through discipline and ordeal... Much of what has been bound by social structure is liberated... (1979, p.149, quoted in McLaren, 1986, p.259).

We can see in this state of being both potential catastrophe and hope. It may therefore be a factor in Giddens' conception of radical modernity, as discussed in chapter 3, comprising as it does both risk and opportunity, tragedy and ecstasy (Berger, 1971). In Turner's original treatment of the process, hope was realised in 'communitas', a 'relationship between concrete, idiosyncratic individuals stripped of both status and role' (Musgrove, 1977: 155); a kind of 'antistructure' – a 'state of undifferentiated, homogeneous human kindness' (McLaren, 1986: 259). There is something magical about it and both intensely real and intensely unreal. Latent or suppressed feelings, abilities, thoughts, aspirations are suddenly set free (Woods, 1993). New persons are born. We found something of this in our teachers (Marcus talked of 'rebirthing'), though we must take care not to exaggerate. Scheduled status passages, like transfer from primary to secondary school, starting work or becoming a parent, all have historically and socially validated emotions that more clearly run the full gamut from risk to opportunity. In unscheduled passages involving, for example, divorce, redundancy, serious illness, the individual has to work harder, the risks may be greater, the opportunities less clear, and the costs can outweigh the rewards.

But before re-birthing there was more levelling and ordeal to come, as 'life in and out of school became complete and utter hell' (Sally). Teachers experienced the absolute rock bottom of despair (the positive side of which is that the only way to go from there is up), followed by a cocooning phase, the prime requisite for the reflexive self in reconstruction; the influence of significant others began to have a beneficial effect in first cushioning and then re-empowering the self; some 'bridging activities' to re-engagement with the outside world followed, with some experimental, though faltering, attempts at identity reconstruction, helped by certain role modifications.

Hitting rock bottom

In spite of the catalogue of problems in the separation phase, actual emotional breakdown typically came as a complete surprise. Celia, for example, thought she was 'coping fine':

> I was doing all the work. The classes were responding without being difficult. They were enjoying the work. Management had observed many lessons, and had been very pleased. Outwardly I was very on top.

However, one day in a staff meeting:

> It was as if my colleagues were talking Chinese. I didn't understand a word they were saying. I couldn't stop crying and had to leave. It was like a piece of elastic and it snapped, as instant as that, one minute, 'Isn't everything fine?' The next minute I was in the doctor's. I couldn't stop crying. I got worse and worse. Nothing had happened but I felt desperate. It had come out of nowhere.

Such panic attacks were a common precipitator, typically triggered by emotional social transactions. Luke's was initiated by his girlfriend's refusal to renew their relationship:

> I was overwhelmed; felt I was going to die. It was the whole emotional release. I was hallucinating. I was a completely different personality. I'd

> thought I'd got a connection to the Devil. I was uncontrollable, my behaviour completely bizarre. Anyone coming near me, I thought they were putting things under my skin. It was so frightening. The walls are moving, the floor's moving, your whole body. It didn't feel like I was me, like there was someone else in my body.

Luke's total bodily shut-down and a short period of psychosis kept him away from work for nine months.

Charlotte's breakdown was sparked off by a school play which 'all went pear-shaped'. Post-amalgamation and with no consultation, Charlotte's working conditions changed and instead of a classroom, the stage in the main hall was designated as her work area for drama. When the hall was in use, she had to spend energy finding alternative accommodation for her students, often at short notice:

> I was trying to move all my GCSE folders in the cabinet that they had bolted to the floor with the set. I didn't realise it was bolted. I was trying to lift it. I had a panic attack. I thought I was having a heart attack. I just walked out, got in my car and went home. It was weird, really weird, like I was floating and didn't know who I was. I'd done something crazy, just walked out. What am I going to do now? Well, I can't go back. I'll just sit here. Wait and see what happens. And of course the phone started ringing, and I didn't answer it. I started really panicking, saying what have I done? Are they going to sack me now? I shouldn't have left those kids, just walking, just going.

Rebecca's narrative illustrates how the perceived 'need to protect the school' may leave teachers open to further harm. After she had endured the sexual assault, as described in chapter 1, 'my acting head didn't want there to be a big ruction, which I understand, wanted to keep it internal, all very hush-hush'. When she returned to school, Rebecca found that no steps had been taken to protect her from further harassment. The perpetrator of the initial incident, initially 'suspended for a couple of days', was placed in isolation in the corridor outside the staff room. Managing the emotional demands of daily encounters with him increased her emotional trauma. 'I hated when I had to see him. It's as if he got away with it, which he essentially did'. In a closed community where such problems were not discussed openly, 'speculation' by the other children 'was a real worry'. A second incident occurred soon after Rebecca's return where a boy asked for his work to be proofread, and 'threw his book full of obscenities about rogering, rape, male rape, from top to bottom down on the table.' As she read this, she found it difficult to manage her emotions and felt her 'face get really red'. She thought she 'was going to burst into tears' as the children 'were all watching me, the other kids on the table, all watching my reaction'. In the staffroom, Rebecca 'burst into tears, lost it, just flipped over'. Her acting Head could not deal with the emotions unleashed by this incident. Rebecca was told to drive home – in this dangerous emotional state – and see her doctor. The episode triggered her total emotional breakdown and Post Traumatic Stress Disorder.

Others collapsed in doctors' surgeries. Gareth, for example, while talking to his GP,

> ... burst into tears – yet another evidence to me that I'd lost control. I felt I'd lost control at school, and there I had lost control of my emotions, all the emotional stress welling up in me. It all spilled out in an uncontrollable way and emotionally I cracked. I broke. I was weeping.

It was Andrew's doctor who recognised that Andrew 'couldn't cope. I was falling to pieces. It was a dangerous situation. I was feeling suicidal'.

Some of the teachers, such as Ralph, Stephen and Jessica, had breakdowns that went unseen because they happened during vacations. Jessica, for example,

> ... spent the first three, four days of that summer holiday crying ... The last week was absolutely horrendous ... I went back in for the training day on the first day and I couldn't control myself, just blubbering all over the place. I went to see the member of the senior management team responsible for staff, sat and sobbed my heart out at the end of the day and I said I just can't come back. (Jessica)

Stephen's holiday at a country cottage with his wife and friends was

> ... total disaster. I just withdrew completely inside my shell. I barely talked to anyone. My wife tried to jolly me out of it, then left me to stew in my own juice. We just fell apart and drifted, totally introverted.

Several of our teachers experienced complete bodily failure at first. Stephen reported

> ... a total blank, like a zombie. I slept most of the day as well as the night, a drug-induced stupor. I was somewhere pretty close to the bottom if not at the bottom, and I stayed there quite a long time.

'It was a nothingness time, limbo' (William). The teachers found it difficult to describe this stage. Andrew, for example, had 'no recollection of that length of time because nothing happened. It's as though the eight weeks didn't exist. *I* didn't exist!' His wife Sarah described him spending the time, 'withdrawn and morose. He sat there in this chair for hours doing absolutely nothing, like a vegetable'. Luke became

> ... completely comatose. Couldn't move my body at all, couldn't get out of bed, complete shutdown. Then I went completely into myself and I didn't care. I suppose I was like that three or four weeks, or maybe it was just two or three days. I had no memory of time. It just seemed forever. Then my body came back. It was uncontrollable, like Tourettes. I was very scared. I felt confused, a complete waste of space. I thought it was my fault all along.

Feelings of despair grew during this early stage of the transitional cycle. Gareth 'became even more depressed because I could not see what would happen to me', while Andrew 'got very despondent, beginning to think very negatively that perhaps I couldn't do the job any more'. Charlotte described this period of depression as having

> ... spikes and it's going to get me. I'm a very happy person deep down inside. It just can't get out. It's stuck. I don't know who it is. I haven't got a clue who I am. I've lost myself somewhere.

It was also a lonely time, during which being removed from social structures cut them off from crucial support networks. In Rebecca's case, her acting Head, who had little expertise in managing a potentially litigious situation properly, one that was 'an extra hassle to him, very bad for the school', silenced her and isolated her from the school support networks she needed at this crucial period because of his over-riding concern to remove Rebecca from the situation.

> He said: 'Contact your union. I'll contact mine. We'll be in touch. It's going to be difficult because I can't speak to you directly. We'll probably seem as if we're on different sides, you getting advice from your union for your protection, me getting advice from mine. Don't

> think I'm neglecting you, if I'm not directly in touch, but this is going to be operational' ... I couldn't speak about it. Colleagues didn't know what had happened. I felt very cut off.

Luke 'couldn't face people seeing what I was like'. Andrew 'didn't want to see people. There were very few I thought I could talk to'.

It can be difficult for someone at 'rock bottom' to find help because they are so depleted of energy and self-awareness. These teachers could not read relevant self-help books. Rachel described the condition:

> ... pains moving around the body, my eyes hurting, shaking, shaking, not able to think for myself, make decisions. I needed to talk but it takes a lot to pick up the phone when you get to that stage. I couldn't go out and see anybody for three months. It took six months at least to be able to sleep properly ... eighteen months before I could read a book.

This, then, was the first stage of the liminal phase of the status passage when teachers were betwixt and between, but to them it seemed as if they were nowhere. Stripped of status and authority, they experienced 'degradation, abasement and humility, a sense of reaching the limit, and 'hitting rock bottom' with reality unstable and in disarray' (Musgrove, 1977: 223). Our teachers testify to disorientation, anomie, loss of identity, loss of control, and the sheer agonies of falling apart. However, while liminality, or marginality as Berger (1971) calls it, involves 'standing outside the taken-for-grantedness of everyday life', which can be terrifying, it can also be sublime, in that new and possibly more fulfilling identities might be forged out of the chaos (see McLaren, 1986: 236-7).

Cocooning

The origins of these new identities arose in cocooning, which involved 'turning inward to take stock, to find your own basic values, and to disengage emotionally and mentally from the life structure' (Hudson, 1991:69); or as Giddens (1991:40) describes it, 'a bracketing, on the level of practice, of possible events which could threaten the bodily or psychological integrity of the agent'. Once the torment of loss could be discarded and emotional stability regained, the mind could be brought to bear on reconstruction.

The teachers identified their need for a moratorium. 'I had to give myself space to have a bit of breakdown' (Celia). Rebecca needed to be a 'recluse'. Margot wanted to

> ... enter a convent. If it hadn't been for me having children I would have. I'd have been quite happy not to speak to anybody. At that stage that's all I wanted – to be locked away in a cell, me, and God, and the Bible'.

Such a moratorium was helpful in providing a grieving period for the loss of both the past and the anticipated future (Kubler-Ross, 1975). Gareth felt 'a grieving there because I was leaving something that basically I loved, teaching. I felt devastated. I thought: 'My life is ended''. For Maureen the stress experience was 'like grief. I equate it with the bereavement process. It's not a personal loss. It's a way of life you've lost'.

A time for reflection gradually presented itself, a time to undertake identity work (Strauss *et al*, 1985). Margot describes valuing

> ... time just for myself, when I wasn't in charge of kids or my own family, time to sit and actually really think about me ... There should be time in your life when you have time to stare: 'What is this life but full of care, we have no time to stand and stare'. I didn't have that. For 18 years I didn't have that. Then all of a sudden I was at home. I was ill. I had time to think: 'Hey! Where am I going from here?'

Alex spent hours walking round and round his housing estate in the snow, analysing the past, pondering his future. Coming to terms with bodily failure created temporary doubts over emotional and mental resilience, and acceptance of being a member of a stigmatised vulnerable group. Marcus 'feared ending up in a looney bin. I had to face the fact that it was a mental thing rather than a physical thing'. Andrew felt

> ... more emotionally vulnerable. It can happen to me. It's not something that only happens to others. In some ways I compare it with physical problems, like I dislocated my shoulder once. This shoulder will never be as strong again. There's nothing I can do about it. Maybe mentally I could be the same way. I'm never going to be quite as strong as before.

Recovery involved understanding the constraints that operated, and the challenges of objectifying the self to obtain insight. In Charlotte's words:

> That's scary because I know I've to start right from point one. First of all, it's got to be therapy for myself to find out, like you do with kids, where am I? Which bits do I want? Which bits are me? Which bits were thrust upon me? I want what I was born to, not what was thrust on me. They can take that back ... The biggest shock of all is seeing yourself, what you really are.

Time out was important so as 'to recover and make sensible decisions' (Luke), facilitate mending and the processes of healing and of reassembling the biography (Strauss, 1987).

> It's important to find yourself back where you were in the past, to let time pass before you make your next move, not to leave, not to run ... I could go in and not have any ghosts in the cupboard. (Luke)

The conscious decision temporarily to abandon social life, to steer clear of emotional experiences, whether negative or positive, helped the teachers to avoid emotive dissonance. Maureen, for example,

> ... deliberately chose to withdraw from the world. I need to be let be for a bit, to come back to the person I know I am. All I want is a choosing-what-I'm-going-to-do day, nothing cataclysmic happening, avoiding anything stressful I can see coming ... I'm in this cocoon I've invented. When I gave up teaching, I wanted to be a recluse. It's my own therapy, my way of coping, my bridging thing, giving myself challenges I can cope with, because they're in my own sphere. I'm in control.

Here is a statement that clearly indicates the beginning of recovery of personal control. Personal choice, positive emotions, the recovery of confidence and self-esteem are beginning to surface.

Taking stock increased self-knowledge and heightened emotional self-awareness:

> Soul searching takes an incredible amount of time. I got really involved in my own understanding. What was making me tick? ...Things I'd been taught, inherited from my mother, the work ethos...Why am I feeling like this?... It's not my fault. I hadn't really respected myself enough. I'd allowed people to take so much from me but I hadn't allowed anyone to put things back. (Margot)

Here we see the early stages of recovery of self-esteem, the assuaging of the sense of guilt and shame, and the initial stages of reassembling the biography (Strauss, 1987). However, few of our teachers, as in Strauss (1987), accomplished this process alone. Social realities were challenged and their awareness developed through transactions with others.

The Beginnings of Reconstruction: the influence of significant others

By the time our teachers sought help they were suffering profound psychological pain. In such a position people are desperately dependent on the work of others; they need temporary social structures, holding environments that provide safety, acceptance and toleration (Hudson, 1991). Extensive support systems are required that provide human and material resources to facilitate the revitalisation of emotional, mental and physical health. As Ralph declared. 'once you've disappeared under the stress fog, it takes somebody from outside to say: 'You've got to stop. You've gone far too far". Charlotte described herself as 'a fallen angel. One that needed her wings tidying up and held'.

In the task of reconstruction, significant others had a vital role (see also Hudson, 1991; Berger *et al*, 1973). Luke managed to recover 'with everybody's help'. His psychiatric nurse told him:

> 'If you can't see any hope you're not going to get better, and you only see hope by people coming around and supporting you' ... It was a process, like hands coming out, people so kind in helping towards the light.

The influence of significant others was first felt during liminality as laying the foundations for reconstruction, and continued into the upward spiral. Significant others were of two kinds, personal and intimate, or professional and distantly expert. The two main functions they provided were, first, a degree of social cushioning for the damaged self; and secondly, raising the awareness of the person recovering so that they could begin the task of re-empowering the self.

Their partners provided emotional support and understanding on the personal side, and the occasional shaft of insight that inspired new realisations. Partners who had themselves experienced stress were more adept at recognition. Ralph's wife Alison

> ... had a bout of stress herself two or three years ago. She was saying: 'Do you realise you're doing the following things?' And of course the answer was 'No'.

Margot's husband Stuart challenged her self-awareness:

> When I discovered what this was, it didn't sink in. The consultant told me it was stress, a dysfunction of the jaw. Later that night I said to Stuart: 'He says I've to wear the guard for six weeks'. Stuart said: 'Yes. That's right'. I said: 'It's day and night. How am I going to teach?' He turned to me and I remember the look. He said: 'What are you talking about Margot? You cannot teach. You can't go back for six weeks'. Up till that stage, it hadn't hit me.

Gareth's wife Marjorie accompanied him to his GP. 'I looked at the expression on Marjorie's face as I was talking. That in part moved me to tears because I saw how all I'd been describing was affecting her'. Partners were instrumental in recognising distress, both seeking medical advice and ensuring that the teachers complied with it. Andrew's wife Sarah, for example, saw he had 'reached crisis point. Saw I was emotionally distressed. Saw it was time the doctor intervened'.

Although some family environments had been a source of stress (see chapter 2), once crisis point was reached they served as therapeutic environments for some of the teachers. Individual family members assumed protective roles. Rachel's husband Matthew had been chronically ill for many years but now Rachel occupied the illness role. Their daughter Hannah described 'role reversals' as Matthew took over Rachel's former roles, becoming the gatekeeper to family interactions with Rachel and the manager of the children's emotions and actions. Hannah protected both her parents, managing her own and others' emotional states, biting back things she would normally have said, being careful how she treated them both. Families reduced the demands on the recovering member and encouraged their removal from stressful situations. Ralph's family, for example, made 'policy decisions' at family meetings to create solitude for Ralph, giving him time and space for reflexivity. Some partners, however, felt they were unsuccessful. Jessica's husband Frank 'tried very strongly to act as gatekeeper', telling the children, 'Leave her alone. Give her time' but if he found they'd gone to her, he exacerbated the tensions. 'I'd jump all over them, making the situation worse'. This further increased the strains within the family and added to spillover effects.

Very few of our teachers gained any positive emotional experiences from their schools during this period. At Walton Green, deputy head Yvonne was 'the only person who actually came and said 'What can we do to help?' (Margot). Alex described Yvonne as 'an angel. She phoned me every day'. Marcus' headteacher acknowledged the role illness plays in life and the need for space to allow the body to recover.

> As soon as the doctor said I was suffering from stress, then she said: I've got Stress at Work's telephone number for you if you want to ring ...Later she asked how things were going. She didn't hassle me, didn't say 'When are you coming back? We've got to think of a replacement'. She didn't put me under any pressure.

Luke 'had cards from the kids. They wrote letters to me, sent chocolates'.

While the creative use of social support systems provides an effective mechanism for both prevention and management of burnout, most organisations, for a variety of reasons, do not make full use of this valuable resource (Pines *et al*, 1981). Our teachers typically reported that their schools had poor informal and formal support provision for teachers suffering stress. Stephen, for example, saw no colleagues during the six months he was ill other than another teacher who was also off ill, and his union representative. 'Neither of the departmental heads that I worked for phoned me up or came in at all. It was as though I didn't exist. I certainly would have expected one of the heads of department, deputy heads, to make contact'. For women in particular, social networks in their working environments can be crucial in maintaining and repairing identity and emotional capital (Bulan *et al*, 1997). For some of the teachers, such as Emily and Charlotte, the loss of prized social networks could not be overcome.

The second kind of significant other is symptomatic of the influence of expert systems in the modern world, one feature of what Giddens (1991: 18) calls 'disembedding mechanisms'. He means by this 'the 'lifting out' of social relations from local contexts and their re-articulation across indefinite tracts of time-space' (*ibid.*) Expert systems 'bracket time and space through deploying modes of technical knowledge which have validity independent of the practitioners and clients who make use of them' (*ibid.*) Interestingly, Giddens identifies the most distinctive connection between expert systems and the self as being evidenced in the development of modes of therapy and counselling (p.33). Giddens sees this as therapy not just to allay anxiety but as a reflection of the reflexivity of the self, carrying both opportunity and risk. This is bourne out in our stress research, where we found that doctors and counsellors enabled some of the teachers to distance their stress and its causes from their personal selves and to situate it within broader social movements and institutions (see also Troman and Woods, 2001).

Doctors provided the diagnosis of stress-related illness, which is important in providing explanations for bodily dysfunction. 'My doctor immediately said this was depression. So it was chemically acknowledged and recognised' (Edward). Charlotte's psychiatrist gave her reassurance by telling her her depression was 'reactive, not endogenous'. Marcus felt the medical recognition gave him 'a justification for feeling that way. I was therefore less likely to rush back to work earlier than I should have done'. Terence was made aware of the life-threatening nature of his distress:

> He took my blood pressure, saw my record on diabetes control. Then he said: 'Without question unless you take this three month break, at least a three month break, you will be dead!'

The doctors validated feelings, legitimated time out for rest away from school, and gave advice solely in the interests of their patients' health and welfare. This gave some an element of instant relief: 'That evening I started to feel better' (Terence).

Eight of our teachers found counselling invaluable for enhancing their understanding of stress emotions and aiding their 're-birthing'. The most beneficial counselling was that which explored both their present and past, revealing unresolved grief, anger and loss. Rachel's counsellor, for example, 'initially treated it as bereavement counselling, got me to think about Dad, and things that hurt'. For Jonathon, counselling 'was the most essential thing that happened':

> I was at rock bottom, partly due to, 'Where the hell's this career going? Do I really want to have a career?' It saved me, saved my bacon, sorted the poor tormented mind. It got me to be level-headed about the past, things gnawing away at me – the maggots. It's allowed me to cope with it, reflect, calm down and go in to school.

Counselling helped Marcus come to terms with a divorce that happened fifteen years before.

> It made me realise that if I could do that with something that had bugged me for fifteen years, I can do the same thing with this situation. Having got rid of that, it left me space to sort other things.

Ralph appreciated that 'anyone can suffer from stress', while Rebecca 'learned to accept it. I opened up a bit, and could see how I had got into such a state'. She came to understand her own 'feeling rules' for keeping herself safe, saying,

> ... I couldn't cry for years, afraid if I cried or let any emotions out, I suppose I had so much to cover, that it would come out like an explosion and I wouldn't be able to get the lid on, wouldn't be able to function.

The counselling process the teachers underwent enabled them to make a comparative analysis of similar emotional experiences over their life history, discovering some elements of consistency among them, thus helping them to theorise about their own experiences and to enhance their emotional literacy. It is acting as a 'disembedding mechanism'.

Increasing self-awareness was a distressing process. 'Initially it destroyed me. It actually makes it worse. It was very painful, what you had to go through to get to the other side' (Jonathon). 'It was a battle because emotions made me scared' (Luke). Alex found it 'hard. The second session I felt a lot easier. Tackling the same issue, I was still in tears'. It was important to these teachers that counselling occurred in a safe environment unconnected to school or home. 'It allowed me to talk to someone who didn't know me, going where you knew it was totally unthreatening, wasn't going to go any further' (Jonathon). Rachel

> ... did a lot of crying. It was very good to be able to do that in private. I couldn't cry in front of Matthew. He would have been hurt. You know that person is going to forget about it. They're not going to take it home with them. You can say things you wouldn't say to anyone else.

Counselling helped distance the self from the stress. 'It threw open doors, made me think, look at myself without being super- or hyper-critical. There's a need to be honest, see ourselves as others see us' (Ralph). 'It made me think about emotions' (Marcus). Counselling helped Marcus see that his stress was not his fault, that some of the children he was dealing with had long-standing emotional and social problems that he, as an individual, was in no position to solve. 'He tried to get me to see things from a different point of view'. Similarly, Rebecca learned that 'there are some things that are totally beyond your control however hard you struggle with them'. 'When you're feeling grotty, you can't see it. My counsellor challenged some irrational thoughts' (Rachel).

Counselling allowed greater understanding of how structures within the school impacted on the stress career. Jonathon found counselling

> ... made what I'm doing more difficult. Made me think of some of the crap you get in this job ... You're given a lot of responsibility but not the authority to go with it, no management structure to support you ... Helps you identify the weaknesses (within the organisation). How we communicate with each other ... the bullying, democratic dictatorship, and poor management ... more discommunication ... how we're losing sight of the kids ... that we've lost ownership at grassroots level.

The counselling is operating here in the interests of the individual whereas in some circumstances it may more directly serve the interests of the organisation. It is enabling the teachers to recognise faults in their organisations. It is helping to lift them out of an individual frame and to re-centre their selves within a set of personal, social, historical and political circumstances. It has moreover helped the teachers relate their emotions to their experiences within these circumstances.

Not all the counselling took this form, nor was all successful. Sally felt the proffered counselling failed to tackle core perceived organisational causes of stress-related illness, and therefore 'missed the point. They need time and motion studies'. Stephen abandoned counselling because he felt that organisational issues were not addressed, his health was not improving. Emily's workplace counselling focused solely on individual strategies in the workplace, for example that she take responsibility for improving her written communication with colleagues. This 'wasn't what I was after. I wanted to talk about relationships and feelings. The counsellor didn't want to talk about relationships and feelings at all'. Emily later found more appropriate counselling privately. Individuals thus engaged with counselling actively, in some cases benefiting from the reconstruction of their identity, in others rejecting it where it was felt to be counter-productive.

Trade unions offered their expertise to some of the teachers. Union representatives provided support at internal grievance procedures and disciplinary hearings. They encouraged the collection of evidence regarding work abuse claims for possible legal action. But Andrew, Margot, Ralph, Terence, Sally and Jessica all found the requirement to obtain and produce documentation a further drain on emotional energies:

> It was as though you were going to be tried for something and trying to prove your innocence. I started gathering evidence, going through files, warfare almost. I thought why should I be doing this? That in itself was making me concentrate less on my job, and more on keeping them from stabbing me in the back, in preparation in case I was taken to the governors again. (Andrew)

For others, union involvement enhanced emotional understanding and legitimated their feelings and actions. Terence's wife Alicia, for example, when discussing potential litigation against his school, began 'to see more realistically how much stress there had been around him, becoming slightly less occupied with who was right and who was wrong'. Andrew's union representative helped his wife Sarah to understand matters, explaining how management were 'making him suffer' (Sarah), and how this would further compromise his competence.

The stress literature is another expert system with which some of the teachers interacted. Individualised stress discourses permeated narratives. Previously, these teachers, their families and colleagues, had believed that stress signalled personal frailty:

> It seemed to affect a lot of women [teachers] I knew, very strong people. I started to wonder if it was their age, but up until that point I hadn't believed it was stress. I thought it was some other weakness in them. (Margot)

These entrenched beliefs were key to hindering effective therapeutic action and apportioning blame. 'It's mostly people who're weak. If you're strong, you can chill it out' (Charlotte). Alex 'was letting [his] partner down. She saw this as weakness'. 'If something goes wrong, I usually think it's my fault' (Luke). Celia felt she'd 'failed completely. My life was in tatters'. Much stress discourse engenders the belief that only certain personality types suffer stress-related problems. '[Colleagues] said, 'We'd never have thought you'd be like that. We didn't think that was your personality'' (Luke). Rebecca 'felt it was external, didn't feel it came from within me. I don't think I'm a depressive character'.

Stress literature helped some of the teachers to 'see it wasn't their fault'. Ralph realised 'anyone can suffer from stress', while, for Maureen,

> ... it made me feel less guilty. I could see some things I was blaming myself for weren't my responsibility. It didn't make the situation any better in changing it to make it easier for me, but it made it easier for me to see that some things I felt were going badly wrong, I'd got no control over.

Several of them showed Denise books they had bought and described what they had learnt from reading them. Jessica, for example, had felt responsible for her stressful relationship with her Head of Department: 'you began to think there was something wrong with you', but research into stress discourses led her to believe that work abuse was endemic in the school system, that acute and chronic scapegoating created fear and anxiety, contributing to the stress cascade.

'We are not what we are', states Giddens (1991: 75), 'but what we make of ourselves ... What the individual becomes is dependent on the reconstructive endeavours in which he or she engages'. This is not just a matter of understanding oneself better. 'In the settings of modernity, the altered self has to be explored and constructed as part of a reflexive process of connecting personal and social change' (*Ibid*: 33). We can see that this is what our teachers are beginning to do at this stage.

Bridging Activities

The next steps taken were faltering attempts to re-engage with the outside world, and forays of varying success into school and other employment arenas. Firstly, our teachers spent time recovering their physical and emotional health. This was a slow process, 'step by step, just getting out of the house, walking round the garden, to the park' (Luke). Small successes helped the rebuilding of their confidence. Celia's doctor, 'good in giving me small tasks', advised doing only one thing every day. 'He said, one day go for a walk, another day do some washing, another day do the shopping. That will be enough'. Celia 'couldn't believe this. I've always been a rush-around person'. Many increased their physical activity 'in the open air' (Gareth). William, Emily and Charlotte worked on their allotments, 'time to be off-duty, your internal space no longer filled with worrying' (Emily). Marcus spent 'more time outdoors in the garden, riding his bike and swimming, enjoying the fact that I was free'. Taking on the responsibility for household tasks, he relieved his teacher wife's domestic burden. 'I enjoy doing that for her, things which improve our quality of life'. They highlighted the importance of 'pottering about' (Stephen). At this stage they sought a 'breathing space' (Edward), with little responsibility and no contact with groups of teenagers.

Creative identity work became a bridging activity that proved vital in rebuilding self-esteem. Maureen felt that 'home was the place I could pick myself up again and recreate myself', so created an art studio, working on pastel painting, cards, plus beginning plans with calligraphy, seashells, mobiles, and framed pictures. Producing posters for a local church provided

> ... a link with the outside world. I'd got to have some contact that made me feel good about the outside world. It's a challenge. That was my bridging thing, my way of getting my high.

They took up old interests. Terence, for instance, spent hours on philately. They gradually rediscovered their creativity. For Morag, it 'took quite a long time and a lot of courage to actually do my own artwork'. Celia bought a tapestry kit to occupy her evenings, while Charlotte experimented with garden sculptures and 'went to life drawing class for the first time since 1978. It was fantastic'. Writing experiences down was therapeutic, helping the teachers to understand the stress experience while distancing them from it. Alex wrote 'a nasty letter' to his partner, 'but didn't send it'. Sally's 'black comedies' which described typical social transactions within school, objectified her distress.

As recovery progressed, the teachers made increasing contact with the outside world. Sally worked in a friend's restaurant, preparing vegetables. She was soon promoted to 'chief lunchtime waitress!' where she could 'switch off the rest of life'. Celia took a journalism course while Emily became a film 'extra'. Voluntary work was an important feature in regaining a sense of worth. Celia helped a young man with mental health problems develop his basic skills. William became a volunteer with his local Wildlife Trust, clearing areas of overgrown countryside, while Marcus did administrative work for a local sports team, organising tournaments, leagues, committee work, refreshments, and writing newspaper reports.

Once again, family, friends and colleagues played significant roles in facilitating positive emotional experiences. Rachel's husband Matthew, for example, having been through something similar, knew recovery required time, space, support and fun. He created 'normalising' experiences, taking agoraphobic Rachel out. Excursions gradually became more challenging, with opportunities for

> ...being daft. Matthew realised how important it was that (a) I had company, because he'd been through it without company during the day, and (b) that he'd got to keep getting me outside. So long as I could go out with him then I was a stage on.

Normalising involved 'finding the energy to be a human being again, to relate to people better' (Maureen). Families readjusted roles, created time and space, raised awareness levels, and tried to reverse the stress process. When Andrew's wife Sarah, for example, could not convince her husband of his value, she realised that it would need an outsider, so encouraged him to accept help offered by a former colleague, who had a decorating business. Des took him into 'a different world. It wasn't teaching, wasn't responsibility' (Sarah). For Andrew,

> It was an alternative life where I could completely switch off ... I had a blind fear of school. Des wouldn't mention school or teaching. We talked about decorating (laughs). At first I didn't help, just watched. Seeing him doing something, I'd give him a hand. Gradually I was doing things, being thanked, having the work commented on as being good ... The lady whose room we decorated was very pleased. The card said 'Thank you for this wonderful room'. I helped do that. It gave me a bit more confidence back.

Several teachers sought succour from their religious community, Celia's local Methodist Minister's wife was 'very good, because she suffers from depression so I've been able to talk to her about it'.

After Luke had been away from school for six months, his colleagues actively demonstrated his value by encouraging a gradual return to school premises, giving him time, and building his confidence.

> I couldn't face being at school ... Part of the process of getting better was you've got to get out, be able to get in the car, be able to drive, things like co-ordinating movements. Gradually I could go out into the environment that was threatening. I'd go sit in the park. My head of faculty used to walk with me. It took a while to do. I met a colleague from work who lived near school, as close to school as I could get. I was in a really bad state. The pastoral head of house came round. He talked to me. He was a really caring person. That's why I could talk to him ... To get to school I went at weekends. Someone would meet me at school. The Deputy Head came. We'd walk round school, see it's not such a bad place.

Small successes helped in the gradual build-up of the teachers' emotional capital. But this period of recuperation was also daunting,

> ... like a long rubber band. I run off and I run off, and at some point I get pulled back, not right back to the start where I started, because I stretch it, but I was frightened to do that. (Luke)

Early retirement procedures prolonged the emotional distress of some. Rebecca, who took 'a year to go through of talking about it, writing about it, having to go over it all', described the powerlessness of this time as

> ... between the devil and the deep blue sea. I didn't feel like myself at all. I couldn't recognise myself. For a control freak, I've been totally out

> of control for over a year, hanging on by my fingernails. Everything's been pending. You can't refocus. The nearer the decision came, the worse I got instead of better ... Everything hinged on this. You knew it was do or die, very dependent on the outcome. There's nothing you can do, everything's in the hands of other people making decisions about you. You have essentially no say so ... Other people are discussing your case and you're not there.

Emily, after being absent from school for twelve months with irritable bowel syndrome, was at first refused early retirement on the grounds of ill-health:

> The psychologist said I wasn't mentally ill, therefore I couldn't have early retirement on the grounds of ill health. I applied. I was refused. I appealed. I was refused. I appealed again. They must have been so fed up with me that they granted it. There were no reasons, no explanation why they refused the appeal.

Recovery is irregular, with many ups and downs (Buyssen, 1996), 'very zigzaggy, a general upward trend but very jagged and saw-toothed. I might go up two steps and fall down one' (Andrew). Although setbacks created anxiety, confidence gradually returned. As the teachers came to realise they were 'employable', they began 'to take more risks' (Emily). Re-engagement with society had begun.

Experimental Re-engagement

As the teachers experimented with possible new roles, they made many false starts and achieved varying results. 'Making extremely irrational decisions' (Luke) was always a possibility during this phase. Several of our teachers sought 'escape' from their present environment. Alex spoke of 'toying with selling up, going off on the streets. I had no drive to do anything else'. Gareth contemplated 'applying to a garden centre, going on the post'. Charlotte proposed selling up and driving to Bosnia with relief supplies, or buying a van and seeking out her relatives in Eastern Europe. Jonathon pondered opening a bed and breakfast establishment, while Marcus explored possibilities of working for travel companies and translation agencies. Andrew considered 'just driving a van, because it seemed no great pressure'. He then went for an interview for 'selling insurance, but it just wasn't me'. Sally contemplated working in a special unit with small groups of severely emotionally distressed youngsters.

The key dilemmas the recovering people faced during this upward phase were: how to move into positive situations; whether to remain in teaching, either in the same school or within another; or whether to seek alternatives outside the teaching world. They had a choice between making a 'mini-transition', 'minor surgery, with a strategic plan to make the life structure work better' (Hudson, 1991: 69) or a 'life transition', involving 'transformation of the self', usually in a different life structure (*ibid*: 90). It was not an easy decision. Andrew, for example, found 'it difficult to make any real decisions at all', so 'made the decision not to make a decision and to carry on being employed by the school, going back and see how I did'. For some, the cocooning period was cut short by the perceived need to return as soon as possible to school, Alex 'to see if I could do it', Luke thinking 'if I hadn't gone back I would always have been running away'. There was a perceived need to 'make a go of it, to prove to myself that I could do the job' (Andrew).

Fifteen of our teachers opted for 'minor surgery'. They re-engaged with teaching environments for varying periods, armed with plans to reduce stressors within their working environment. The decision to return to teaching was partly influenced by financial considerations. There were mortgages to pay, pensions to secure, children to put through university. Margot's husband Stuart described the 'no win, Catch 22 position', where loss of her income through ill-health would mean losing their home and valued lifestyle, whereas returning to work might jeopardise her health. They also felt guilty both towards their pupils, particularly those preparing for examinations, and towards their already stressed colleagues:

> They do lots of drawing and painting that needs to be continuous. For me to be away just one week is vital to the whole game, that the same person is there and builds that confidence. If I'm away I feel terribly guilty so consequently I'm never ill. I just can't afford to be. (Margot)

Luke had 'such a big hang-up about letting people down at work, embarrassed about the situation I was in' seeing colleagues as 'lumbered, the whole faculty going mad, doing the first National Curriculum SAT test pilot'.

The liminal period was prolonged when teachers returned to schools that were in flux and were sites of frustration and anxiety. Rebuilding emotional capital was difficult, often impossible, in situations which offered no solidarity to develop collective ways of coping, and no flexible systems to support their return. One of the main structural processes that hindered teachers' self-renewal processes was the requirement to return to work full time. Some local authorities and schools refused to grant them a gradual return, starting on a part-time basis. 'They said you're either fit to work or you're not fit to work. If you're fit to work you do full time, if you're not fit to work, you don't work – completely inflexible' (Luke).

The support systems management set up in response to teachers' return proved largely unworkable due to unresolved problems with providing skilled personnel or sustaining organisational resources, and no directed time was allocated to facilitate a commitment to hold preventive and protective measures in place. The initial support Rebecca received on her return to school, for instance, was 'brilliant. Bobby elected to be my 'buddy', my minder. Staff were wonderful, supported me, welcoming me back in, offering to be with me'. But all this ceased within two weeks as colleagues became 'engrossed in workloads', with a second Ofsted inspection and mock SATs looming.

Another difficulty was that professional support might not necessarily be interpreted or received as a benefit, due partly to increasing demands on the returning teacher's time and workload, which made Emily, for example, 'iller'. Stephen, having lost confidence in his classroom management, found his interaction with colleagues just compounded his sense of hopelessness, as 'students wouldn't calm down for them either'.

As it was, the high numbers of teachers requiring assistance generally overloaded the support systems, spreading the stress 'virus' by creating a 'vicious circle, a spiral' where

> ... the more colleagues are out, the more you pull together and try and mop up their work on a temporary basis, but when their absences go into terms, we're talking weeks, then months, you end up doing two people's jobs. (Pauline, Marcus' wife)

As Jonathon observed,

> People don't feel anybody's been able to help. They've papered over the cracks. It seems all right now. Then the person helping has gone on to another problem, left the person to it. That exacerbates the situation. In a very big school like this, it's always moving on to the next train, because it's always coming down the line. You can't afford to spend time in the engine room, because the next one's busy queuing up behind.

One of Teacherline's suggestions is to 'ask for help' from unions. But neither Margot nor Ralph could fulfil their duties as union representatives satisfactorily. 'So many teachers were putting on' Emily's union representative, 'she was practically having a nervous breakdown herself'. Teachers felt constrained in actively seeking help from internal support systems as 'everybody was so busy. You couldn't break down because you knew it would re-arrange the whole schedule' (Rebecca). Similarly, Emily perceived her support needs as

> ... putting pressure on colleagues. Other people had too many problems to be able to help. There was no room for anyone else to be draining their energies. It just adds to the stress, really preyed on my conscience.

Charlotte observed a general lack of 'care' about 'how people were being treated'. But it was not that colleagues simply didn't care. Support systems collapsed under the pressures of educational reform, leading to a widespread view of today's education system as ill equipped to provide support. In Luke's words, 'the way the system's going at the moment, people like myself, would've been chucked on the scrap heap'.

The teachers also felt they needed to manage stigma in their workplace. When people suffer mental and emotional distress, they 'cease to receive positive definitions of themselves from their primary social groups' (Turner, 1987: 73). As Goffman (1964: 57) shows in his analysis of stigma, people expend emotional energy managing both the 'information' about their 'imputed failings', and the 'tension generated in social contacts'. Our teachers reported changes in their perceived and actual status within school, as stigma was attached to the self, not to the situation. Colleagues, family and friends were afraid they might have a relapse. Celia found 'people always looking to see if you're well. Is she OK? Is she going to do anything strange?' Managing minor emotional transactions when they feared these could possibly be read as indicators of stress, increased their emotional labour, as Andrew explained:

> It's not like a physical illness. Before, if I wanted to do something, I did it. Didn't really concern myself too much about it. If people thought I was mad or crazy, I don't care. Now I think more about it. Will this look good? Will this look bad?

Opportunities for increasing positive emotion through workplace activities and for reconstructing positive work identities were hindered by continued intensification of work, the demands of marketisation and financial constraints, league tables and having to implement a range of management initiatives in response to the demands of Ofsted:

> We've changed our school day in order to save money on the budget. We've lost non-contact time. We've had four redundancies this year not replaced, so they're all working harder. (Yvonne, deputy head, Walton Green)

This meant

> ... fewer staff and more pupils, fewer free periods and larger classes than last year, more of those fewer free periods being used up as cover. The workload has increased. I'm finding it difficult to get everything done in the time. (Jonathon)

The demands of constant school improvement resulted in

> ... pressure from the top all the time. You've got to move up. Everyone's running around in a panic. It's got to be better next year or there's going to be trouble. As a mathematician, [I know] it's bound to go up and it's bound to go down. (Luke)

Andrew described

> ... jumping through hoops to satisfy management. The 'D's are being pressurised more than anyone else. They've got to get C's. If anyone gets a 'D', it's my fault. They must be *made* to go to lunchtime revision clubs.

Promises that their working conditions would be modified on their return to work were not always carried through. Gareth's timetable did not change. Teachers reported that their workloads continued to rise, and that they had difficulties maintaining good social relationships. Margot, for example, who was a popular and successful teacher, described herself as 'a victim of my own success'. Because she achieved such a high GCSE pass rate, many low ability children chose her practical subject as an option. But she 'didn't get the promised technician' and continued to feel 'very angry, very upset' at the uneven distribution of the workload within her department, which seemed always to favour her colleague. She had 'fits at school about it', feeling 'terribly bitter that my HoD's deliberately put this timetable upon me, and it comes out. I can't help it'. Structural demands concerning staffing, timetabling difficulties and financial constraints did nothing to ameliorate her emotional trauma. Margot was starting to think

> ... I've got on top of these emotions. I'm really coming out of this. Next year, they've lumbered me with a timetable that's twice as hard to run as last year, even though I was ill last year, more paperwork, more marking, lots of problems trying to keep in contact with other teachers. They're adding more burdens. Yesterday I cried all afternoon, in a right stress. I couldn't sleep again.

Recovery was difficult in environments like these:

> I don't know how I'm going to get through it. I've asked for help. I've done everything this pamphlet has told me to do. Please take some of this burden away from me! (Margot)

In pressured environments of this kind, the teachers adjusted their lives and developed coping strategies while at the same time seeking ways to reconstruct their identities.

Role Modifications

Some of our teachers removed themselves from aspects of their teaching environments they perceived as contributing to negative emotion, while remaining in the same school. For Ralph, Luke, Celia, Charlotte and Jonathon, this involved *downshifting*, meaning giving up particular responsibilities. Luke's Head of Faculty took over 'all the managerial side. I was just doing a teaching job, no form, no groundbreaking education, and no responsibilities'. Jonathon's 'career aspirations dropped amazingly'. One difficulty he had in his promoted post was discord with his colleagues. He decided that the classroom was a 'safe environment', so took a 'demotion', relinquishing his responsibilities for GNVQ co-ordination. He explained: 'I don't want to have to deal with conflict, don't want to have to play that game any more'. He reported that his decision was unpopular with management, that a secretary told him: 'Your name is mud'. Ralph, however, received positive comments from colleagues when he gave up the responsibilities of Head of Year. Nonetheless, downshifting proved to be a 'two-edged sword' (Edward) that could involve 'losing face' (Jonathan):

> I've rationalised my future. That creates a sort of stress. There's no turning back. It's frustrating because part of me knows I could do a senior teacher job ... Saying 'No' actually creates more stress because you're not doing enough to make your job fulfilling. I'm not working on all four gas burners. The energy banks aren't there. It's a big stress factor. (Jonathon)

Taking on part-time peripatetic supply violin teaching was 'quite a triumph' for Celia,

> ... a big step forward in that I'm able to go into school. It's been better for my family, four days a week, 9 till 2, small groups or one-to-one, very low pressure, which suits me, no preparation. You're just in and out. It's like guerilla warfare.

Downshifting also affected financial security. Part-time working reduced pension funds and it did not always radically reduce workloads.

> It's: 'Let's reduce the timetable'. I found out really that it wasn't enough because I just lost my frees. I needed to have a whole day being away from family, away from school ... I feel worried because I'm broke. (Charlotte)

Emily thought her Head's suggestion that she accept a part-time contract would not be helpful, as she would still have to deal with interpersonal conflicts within the department.

Stephen's headteacher proposed *role-redefinition* (Troman and Woods, 2001) as a temporary solution to Stephen's problems.

Finding it difficult to replace Stephen's IT skills due to impending school closure, he re-employed Stephen on a temporary part-time basis as an IT technician because Stephen was 'the only person who knew personally how to work the computer systems'. Stephen was able to avoid negative transactions with students by dropping his teaching tasks, while still retaining some of the computing he previously enjoyed, so the new role created opportunities to increase his feelings of competence and self-worth. He no longer had to manage his own emotion or those of the children in the classroom. He was able to separate spheres, to balance work and home lives:

> I have a lot more choice. I don't bring any work home with me unless I want to. Frequently I'm working in classrooms where children are being difficult. It's not my problem. I don't even have to stay in the room if I don't want to.

Some teachers redefined their role in unofficial ways. Withholding criticism and avoiding 'upsetting the applecart' was a common strategy. Jonathon was

> ... not as brutal, as spade-is-a-spade as I used to be. I go to meetings, and put my hands under my knees, saying: 'Don't talk. Don't talk'. That's hard for me! I'm quite opinionated.

Alex adopted a similar approach: 'I'm being careful now. That's a shame, because by being careful, I'm not saying a lot of things that need to be said'. He ceased confronting colleagues:

> It's difficult to do things at work that I want to do. It's too much out of my control. I'll carry 'deadwood' very supportively if there's only a small number of people in that position. But when the majority are like that, it's hard. My strategy is to ease off on expectations. Put things in perspective.

Most of the teachers *changed their commitment* to teaching in some way. For Ralph, teaching 'used to be a vocation. Now it's just a job'. During the separation phase, they experienced this as a loss. Now they have settled for it. During this liminal stage, Margot changed her sense of commitment from the vocational to the instrumental:

> It's just a job. I'm getting paid for it. I'm not getting the big thrills I got out of it. I'm prepared to do it as long as I have to. If I could get out, I don't think I would give it a second look back.

These modifications were often viewed as temporary measures, designed to give further breathing space and to explore options while receiving an income. Jessica, for example, was 'trying very hard to leave from a job to a job'. Alex, however, maintained both 'professional' and 'vocational' commitments, believing his job to be 'more important than anything else'. He saw his role as 'training to be a manager. It's a bit like teaching practice'. He planned to 'bide my time, keep my nose clean, get the reference and basically move on'. Like some of the others, he felt trapped, viewing his high salary as a drawback. 'They can have college leavers cheaper than me'.

For the majority of these teachers, school processes prolonged the liminality period. Jessica and Andrew both found sustained abusive transactions in the original school environment continuing to attack their identity. Jessica felt increasingly incompetent as departmental emotional politics persistently surrounded her.

> It's like victimisation ...You can shut Patricia up for a while by standing up to her but to stand up to her, you've got to be on your toes all the time, thinking about what she's saying, what she's doing. I don't want to be like that. I want to be doing my job rather than thinking how to defend myself or stand up to her. It's not the way I work. I needed to take some action against her. I'd already done that once and I just couldn't face doing it again.

Departmental rivalry and negative emotion increased. Valued colleagues left. Collegial relations were lost. The burdens of carrying out emotional labour with their family, colleagues and students took further tolls on the teachers' well-being. Jessica 'didn't really know whether teaching was what I wanted to do. It had undermined me so much I didn't think I was a good teacher any more'.

Conclusion

This chapter describes the experience of transition in a status passage. There is the emotional turmoil involved in the separation of self from structure: ordeal, torture, panic and disorientation as status, authority and identity are felt to be stripped away. But our teachers also experienced liberation from social structure, liberation from assigned identities and positions and careers that might have become out of synchronism with their essential selves. We see the teachers reaching rock bottom, but in time, through cocooning, by distancing themselves from torment and finding space for the necessary process of grieving over lost selves (Nias, 1991), we see them beginning identity work and recovery of the self, and reaching new emotional understanding. Significant others helped in the social cushioning and re-empowering of the self, raising awareness, providing social contextualising for their stress, assuaging the teachers' sense of guilt and blame. Our teachers gradually recovered their physical and emotional health, rediscovered their creativity and began to re-engage with the world. They modified their roles to help them through this stage. But recovery was irregular, faltering. There was no smooth passage back to an ideal normality. As re-engagement brought teachers back to the real world, they inevitably faced dilemmas that prevailed in that world and the part they were to play in it. Agonising decisions still had to be made.

In the next chapter, we discuss how some of our teachers successfully negotiated the liminality period, won through the dilemmas and recovered a measure of ontological security.

5

The Reconstruction of Identity

'Burnout signals not despair but hope' write Freudenberger and Richelson (1980: xxi). 'Recognized and attended to, burnout can become a positive energy force, signifying that the time has come for a cease and desist action, a hard look at yourself, and a change to something new'. Pines *et al* (1981: 3) suggest, 'while burnout can be an extraordinarily painful and distressing experience, as with any difficult event, if properly handled it can not only be overcome, it can be the first step towards increased self-awareness, enriched human understanding, and a precursor of important life changes, growth and development. Accordingly, people who have experienced burnout and have overcome it almost invariably end up in a better, fuller, more exciting life space.' To what extent had our teachers been successful in finding a 'more exciting life space' by the conclusion of this research? How far had they managed to re-engage with society and reconstruct their identities?

Self-renewal is an emotional journey whereby people learn to move out of negative situations and into positive ones that satisfy their need for work and love. It entails 'the re-birth of self-esteem, a re-evaluation of core issues and beliefs and the recovery of hope and purpose' (Lankard, 1993: 4). A time 'to *hold on* to what is working in your life, *let go* of what is not working, *take on* new learning and exploration of options, and *move on* to new commitments' (Hudson, 1991: 98), it requires honest reflection and self-assessment, to recognise when change is necessary and overcome fears of the unknown. Characterized by 'periods of acceleration, reversal, setback, plateau, and variation in the boundaries of the limitations' (Strauss, 1987: 226), 'successful self-renewal follows successful cocooning', and restores to the person 'the ability to be self-sustaining, producing confidence, energy, and hope' (Hudson, 1991: 69).

However, as we have seen, not all our teachers successfully negotiated the cocooning period. Not all were renewed in the same way nor to the same level of personal satisfaction. Some felt enhanced in different ways, some felt diminished, some a bit of each. There was no clear pattern. Some of our teachers experienced false renewal. Charlotte's burnout, for example, was so entrenched that she could not recover while in school. Despite being given resources to convert a classroom into a drama studio, she could overcome neither the loss of her previous social network nor the loss of her value system, and subsequently had a further breakdown. We know little about Morag's and Sally's self-renewal journeys because we unfortunately lost touch with them.

Several of our teachers, however, readjusted their goals and expectations. Some cast aside the linear view of the life cycle, adopting a cyclical view which offered a more flexible way of being, more adaptive to societal change, with higher levels of interactivity and emotional resilience. Identity reconstruction was accomplished primarily by means of putting into effect some of the wisdom acquired in the liminal period by making changes in working environments and in the self.

Reinventing Work

As described by Bergquist *et al* (1993: 18), reinventing work was for our teachers a 'central part of reinventing themselves'. During periods of reflection and assessment, 'when you reflect and think: Do I actually want to do this for another fifteen or sixteen years?' (Jonathon), our teachers re-evaluated the extent to which they felt teaching in the current educational climate satisfied their needs. They embarked on analysis: 'What was enjoyable about teaching still? Was it really worth continuing along this road?' (Margot) and explored solutions. They considered how they might adapt to specific teaching environments, and how changes in working environments might contribute to greater fulfilment in life.

But this was not always at the teacher's discretion. Both William and Stephen were warned that competency procedures would be implemented if they insisted on returning to school. As William's wife Lindsey explained, stress exacerbated William's hearing difficulties. His speech became indistinct. His continuing to work in a practical classroom environment with large groups of teenagers raised specific health and safety issues. Stephen was deemed 'unfit to teach' due to long-term stress-related problems, his health likely to become further impaired if he returned to a school environment. Several of the others took the initiative to redirect their own lives and careers. Identity reconstruction was achieved in one of three main ways: returning to the original working environment; relocating to another educational establishment; or rerouteing to some other form of work (See Table 2). We consider each in turn.

Returning

Only three of our teachers found measures of self-renewal through returning to their old posts. This was not a passive acceptance of the new assigned social identity. Margot, for example, was four years later:

> enjoying teaching again. I've learned to say 'No'. I was very much abused, and will make sure I am not abused again. I've a superb timetable next year. Had a marvellous appraisal. It's now:'How can we help? What can we do to keep you?'

She felt confident about her teaching skills. As 'NUT negotiator, dealing with a huge lot of problems', she has gained 'huge respect' for her teaching, 'No-one has better results than me, so I don't have to hold my tongue. I'm not frightened of management, but if I wanted promotion I wouldn't do this union job'. She was able to be proactive in shaping her environment, for example, reducing her workload by writing

> ... a report to my senior management team asking for help. Management were desperate to keep me happy. I spoke to governors. They gave me the technician I asked for. He's a godsend. I now have some SEN help in the classroom, and they let me have a year without a form, to help me get back into it.

Table 2. Characteristics of the sample of teachers at the end of research

Teacher	Self-renewal route	Position at end of research	School location
Jonathon	still in post	Head of Business	Walton Green, urban comprehensive
Margot	still in post	Arts teacher	Walton Green, urban comprehensive
Luke	still in post	Maths, second in department	urban comprehensive
Alex	relocation	Head of Science	town comprehensive
Andrew	resignation, relocation	Science co-ordinator	urban middle school
Charlotte	redundancy, relocation	Drama teacher	urban middle school
Emily	ill-health retirement, relocation	Part-time basic needs teacher	technical college
Jessica	relocation	Home economics teacher	rural comprehensive
Marcus	ill-health retirement, relocation	Part-time French teacher	private school
Celia	resignation, re-routeing	Music therapist	N/A
Edward	early retirement, re-routeing	Manager of sheltered workshop	N/A
Gareth	resignation, re-routeing	Christian ministry	N/A
Maureen	early retirement, re-routeing	Self-employment	N/A
Rachel	ill-health retirement, re-routeing	Self-employment	N/A
Ralph	redundancy, re-routeing	Industry	N/A
Rebecca	ill-health retirement, re-routeing	Self-employment	N/A
Stephen	ill-health retirement, re-routeing	IT co-ordinator	N/A
Terence	ill-health retirement, re-routeing	Charity manager	N/A
William	ill-health retirement, re-routeing	Laboratory technician	N/A
Morag	resignation, re-routeing	unknown	unknown
Sally	resignation	unknown	unknown

Those who embraced aspects of the new teacher identity focused on creating positive emotional climates both in their classrooms and across the school. Luke refused promotion, preferring to remain a 'chalkface' teacher in the same school. With a vocational commitment, he gains great satisfaction at work through his interactions with students. Margot cares less about the breakdown of teaching in her department and is 'more passionate about trying to get the school day right, something everybody could benefit from'. She too gets 'such a buzz' from her students,

> ... such lovely things from the kids out of clay. That's why I've kept going. I get a real thrill out of what they're doing. The work they're doing is so exciting, very experimental. It's brilliant. I love it. When I'm finished, I'm exhausted, but I don't mind that exhaustion.

However, teaching continues to be perceived as

> ... abuse. The only way to think of it is to say: that's management's role and that's my role, and if it gets too much, stop. I won't do it. I won't let it go that far again. Say this is my teaching role. I will push myself to a certain level but as soon as I feel I've had enough, it's stop! Get the hell out! That's the only way to keep your sanity. (Margot)

Jonathon was deeply unhappy about his decision to downshift and felt 'frustrated', 'wasted' and 'blinkered'. He told us: 'I keep banging my head against a brick wall saying it's a vocation, but in reality I'm looking for other vocations to follow'.

Relocating

Other teachers began to recognise that some elements within their life cycle were increasingly dysfunctional and that they needed to make further adjustments to working spheres. In certain negative teaching environments, self-renewal proved impossible due to

> ... more and more pressure. It didn't look as if it was going to get any better. There was going to be continued blame for whatever went wrong. I decided I wasn't going to go on like that. I made the choice. It was resignation. I couldn't see any improvement so I had to get out, left the job I was in without a job to go to. (Andrew)

Marcus 'realised that if I went back to the same school I should be ill. Leaving the situation was very positive on my state of mind and my quality of life'. Others felt powerless to continue to battle against systems they perceived as unable to deal with conflict and change. A measure of financial security allowed some of them greater choice in exploring alternative arenas. William, Stephen, Emily, Rebecca, Marcus and Terence were awarded breakdown pensions, Ralph and Charlotte redundancy. Edward and Maureen accepted early retirement, each having spouses who earned an income. Andrew, Rachel, Morag, Celia, Sally, and Gareth resigned. 'I love teaching but I can't teach in that environment. It's a rotten job' (Sally).

Teachers worried that stigma might reduce their chances of finding alternative employment. Interviews were suffused with anxiety, due to their fears lest 'imputed' weakness would be carried into other employment arenas. 'I'm a bit concerned whether they ask me whether I've ever been depressed when I go for the interview, because that's the sort of question they may ask of someone who wants to work with anybody. I'm a bit concerned about prejudice; whether they'll give me a fair chance' (Celia). However, such fears were largely unfounded and six teachers found new teaching positions.

Andrew did some supply work and soon found a job teaching in a middle school where he feels 'if I can just get on with the job of teaching without constantly looking over my shoulder, then I'm happiest doing that'. Emily found 'respect' teaching basic skills part-time in the local technical college, where her students

> ... are very, very keen. It's bloody marvellous. They know they need those skills. The whole style of teaching is laid back. We treat them as adults, no pressures.

Charlotte, too, ultimately secured a position in a middle school. Alex gained promotion – a HoD post in northern England. Marcus teaches part-time in the private sector, in an 'eccentric' small school with a 'family atmosphere' where he has a great deal of autonomy and almost no administrative duties. He finds the emotional climate in the classroom more congenial to teaching foreign languages. The students accept boundaries. He is no longer engaged in 'crowd control'. There is a good deal of humour:

> Rapport is very good. The kids are wonderful, no stress ... The big thing I enjoy about this school is you can have fun with pupils, talk to them, the older ones particularly, on an adult level, have a laugh and a joke with them'.

Jessica's solution was to accept a post in a smaller comprehensive school. She contrasted her old school environment with the new as 'North and South Poles! Totally different atmospheres'.

Re-routeing

Some of our teachers found self-renewal in any school impossible. Their identity reconstruction was aided by 're-routeing' (Troman and Woods, 2001). Rachel did not 'want to have anything to do with teaching', while Maureen declared a return to school would 'kill' her. 'Because of all the outside factors outside my control, I couldn't recover in school so I felt it was better to take myself out of that situation, and into a situation where I do have control'. Rebecca

> ... felt so panic-stricken, just the prospect of going in, to pick up some files. I was terrified. Even thinking about it I was shaking, causing me such anxiety I couldn't sleep. I couldn't steel myself to do that. Each time I couldn't get through the door. I felt physically nauseous, very frightened by the atmosphere in school. Going back to the room where I taught, and the area where he groped me, I found extremely difficult. Gradually I came to the conclusion that I wouldn't be able to go back to teaching.

Maureen's solution was self-employment, where she was able to pursue her own artistic ventures in the hope of selling her products at craft fairs, 'finding work patterns that leave you time to be human, to do things that really make me tick as a person, establishing myself as an individual artist, listening to music, reading a book!' Time became 'creative' for her, no longer 'the enemy', and work was 'fulfilling the need to be challenged'. Maureen felt she had

> ... discovered the true secret of happiness, not to think too much about the past, not to project yourself too far into the future so you're frightened about what might happen. Make the best of now.

Rebecca and Rachel started their own small businesses, Rachel relocating to the countryside to set up a small art and holiday centre with her husband, while Rebecca returned to her artistic roots 'to get through this sense of loss. My painting is very much my identity'.

Within seven days of obtaining early retirement through ill-health, Terence found employment with a charity, where he has remained for several years and is 'thoroughly enjoying it. It's a whole new ballgame, a different professionalism'. Edward too is working successfully for a charity, creating employment for adults with special needs. His new job accords with his religious ethics: 'I've slotted into something that suits me down to the ground. It just feels right'. He felt 'a whole piece of my life has been put aside but I'm not sad about it. I'm positive about it, excited at the prospect of finding new things I can do'. Celia decided to 'find a life where I can be the primary carer', so she retrained in music therapy, hoping to be 'around the home more for my children because nobody else is going to be around for them'. She had concluded that

> ... I didn't fit in with teaching as a profession because I'm very keen on the individual determining their own path in life, and as a teacher I had very strong ideas about how I wanted to be as a teacher, and I didn't always sit neatly with the establishment. I decided I'd like to still work with people. I've done the Counselling introductory course, so it seemed the natural thing to combine my personal skills and my musical skills.

She felt 'excited by this prospect. I hope in music therapy I'll be able to be myself more and develop more my own way of being!' For Gareth, the end of teaching has been 'a doorway' to another 'joyous' way of life that makes use of his interpersonal skills in the ministry.

For others, like Maureen, Gareth, Terence and Edward, new pathways facilitated their embracing roles that are more in tune with their personal philosophies and values. Jessica finds 'education is more child-centred' in her new school. New environments provided the opportunity to begin again with a clean slate. 'People accept me for what I am and what I can do, rather than having preconceived ideas about me' (Andrew). They also facilitated closure on the agonies and torment of the downward spiral. Rachel's rerouteing allowed both the 'ritual of exiting all teaching materials', and 'cutting off the pain. The last few years were very dead.' She embraces her new life, which 'on the whole, has been joy'. Maureen 'can afford to put the past in its right place'.

Reinventing work, however, was not successful for everyone. Three who remained in teaching had failed to find a 'more exciting life space' in their teaching careers by the time the research ended. They were still to some degree nursing spoiled identities. Andrew, like

Jonathon, did not consider his life fulfilling. 'Before these problems occurred, I was getting people through A levels and to university, a lot more fulfilling than teaching middle school. It hasn't got the risk. It's safe'. Alex continued to have a 'tough ride' in a 'failing' department where he had 'been let down on promises':

> A changed working environment has not improved my well-being. TQM (Total Quality Management) is the guide of my management life. However, education is not TQ, quite the opposite. My job is quick fix, knee jerk. It is very difficult to apply the methodology, and it frustrates me.

Alex remains optimistic, however, and has 'little fear of failure', hoping that within two years his department will be 'sorted, one way or the other'. Morag felt unfulfilled as a shop assistant, as did William as a scientific officer in a laboratory, and both are seeking alternative options. In most instances, though, finding new vocations presented opportunities for reinventing themselves through positive emotional experiences originating in organisational practices that promoted positive emotional climates and higher levels of organisational emotional literacy.

Finding Positive Emotional Experiences

Finding positive elements within emotional climates is crucial to self-renewal; it offers the potential for rebalancing emotional lives and for re-establishing consistency between social identity and self-concept. What was it about these environments that contributed to their feelings of well-being?

Terence reported

> ... this snowballing of an accumulation of positive things, whereas previously, there'd been an accumulation of negative things. Things started to snowball in a positive direction once I had the courage to apply for this job. It increased more once I got the job. It increased more once I'd started it.

In his case, optimism and hope are shaped through positive, 'good' stress:

> People ask: 'How's the job?' I say: 'Great. I love it'. There are tensions. The pressures are on, but it's stress you enjoy ... I have evening meetings twice a week, much longer than school meetings. I don't notice them, because I'm actually enjoying them. (Terence)

For Andrew, a climate of safety and honesty affords positive emotional feelings:

> It's a more honest environment. They're giving you the truth and that makes you feel better. ... You don't find people looking for faults all the time. They are not trying to apportion blame or deflect the blame. I did feel vulnerable at the last school. Any criticism was a personal attack, but now I feel if someone suggests I could do something better, I wouldn't take it so personally, so I don't feel as vulnerable now. I don't have any fears about going in.

Some teachers moved into supportive, trusting, caring, collaborative cultures:

> It's very, very supportive. You could go with a problem and you'd be listened to and helped rather than hindered and blamed. Previously I, and many others, felt that if there was misbehaviour in the classroom, the teacher was failing. Now the blame lies with the pupil. ... There's good liaison between teachers and learning support staff, who here come into the lesson rather than taking the pupil out. (Andrew)

> People are genuinely very friendly. They care. The staff is quite settled, happy. It's got the support of management. They look after each other. I trust them. (Jessica)

> I feel very much at home, a much more relaxed, laid back, friendly, warm atmosphere, people with a will to make it work. That spins off on me. At school there was so much antagonism, many students actively seeking to stop the system working. The positive vibes [here] are a big help. (Edward)

They flourish in environments where people are valued:

> People are respected. You don't need to kow-tow. You treat them with the respect that they hold [of] you. Whether you're a receptionist, a caretaker, a finance manager, the director, if they deserve respect, they get respect. (Terence)

> Nobody raises their voice, or bullies. (Emily)

Their new organisations are typically 'on a more human scale. It's smaller and I know everyone by first names' (Andrew). As noted by Smith (1992), positive emotional climates encouraged higher levels of individual and collective emotional literacy:

Most of this job is developing my strengths. The last few years in school seemed to point out my weaknesses, being asked to do things I wasn't good at. What I was good at wasn't being asked of me. There's an awful lot to learn here but I feel I've the potential for learning what I need to know. (Edward)

I'm more confident about my teaching capability. I'm so much happier in the situation I'm in. I feel valued, not because people pat me on the back but because people will come and speak to me, discuss something with me, say: 'Yes that's good. I like that'. That's it, no great praise. That to me means far more, makes me feel as though I belong, that I'm a valuable part of the department. (Jessica)

Motivation for Terence, Jessica and Andrew is facilitated by sharing common aims and goals with their colleagues.

We're all in the same boat, on the same side. It's the feeling that we're all in it together, working together. You feel people in positions of authority, in management, are facing the same problems, rather than saying you shouldn't be having these problems. It doesn't make the problem go away but it makes you feel better about it. The same problems face all schools. It's just how they're dealt with. There's pressure to get good SAT results, to reduce truancy, to keep the numbers up, but management here isn't trying to deflect that onto staff. They will say, what are we going to about it? It's we, not what are you going to do about it? Totally different. We still have the problem but it's the way it's viewed. It's us and we're in it together. (Andrew)

Work is de-intensified and their autonomy is stronger:

I'm in charge of the budget. I got to design my own lab. I cover the agreed county curriculum but how I do it is up to me. (Andrew)

I decide what I teach. As long as my work fits with the tests, it doesn't matter how I do it. Kids can't do this technological approach to technology without basic skills. My head of faculty is quite happy in Lower School just to put in basic skills although that really isn't what the technology orders are asking for. (Jessica)

I feel more in control. This business is set up within our control, with our decisions. (Rebecca)

There are more democratic management structures:

I know I'm inputting to decisions. Our comments are taken notice of. The final documents take account of our feedback. Our opinions are

> valued. Before it was dictatorship. Here, it's not we've asked you but we're doing it this way anyway, we are consulted. School meetings are democratic. (Andrew)

> My role is changing, being enhanced, with a 25% increase in salary, but through negotiation and agreement. It does my ego the power of good! (Terence)

Jessica, Terence and Andrew all now experience joint decision-making and collegiality:

> My head of faculty asked: 'What do you think about this options booklet, Jessica?' We read it together, changed bits here and there. At the end of the day I sit down with my technician, sort out what we're going to teach. We work as a team. There's more a culture of 'we've got to work together' here. No-one says: 'This isn't my job'. (Jessica)

Hierarchies are flattened:

> There's a hierarchy in any organisation, but it's not as autocratic as in schools. The Head was always the Head. He was the boss. The Deputy was his Deputy. They were more important than the teachers. Despite the changes in society, that structure, even in the most liberal schools, has stuck. You don't get that here. (Terence)

Some enjoy relaxed and good communication and positive staff/student relationships:

> We speak to kids. When my head of faculty wants me to do something there's no pressure. He doesn't treat me as though I'm incapable, stupid, thick. He asks me in the morning how I am, then leaves me alone. He wanders in and out of my lessons and I don't feel threatened. He's wonderful. He might very well be coming to check up on me but tells me a joke at the same time! (Jessica)

> You can talk in the staffroom freely, say what you feel and others will support you rather than you having to be careful about what you said or who was listening at the time. Others are willing to discuss any problems they might be having. (Andrew)

They have no problem with criticism when it is constructive:

> I've had mostly praise yet I don't feel I'm doing anything different to before. I could teach the same lesson in my previous school and in this one and get a totally different appraisal. It would have been below standard. Before, I knew they were going to be critical. Here, senior

> management can come in any time. I don't feel I'm being spied on. No-one's constantly trying to find fault. (Andrew)

Genuinely positive remarks from others are rewarding, Jessica's Head of Careers reportedly said of her: 'She's a good catch. We're lucky to have her'. Jessica 'couldn't believe that anybody had really wanted me that much. That really set me very much on my way'.

Edward and Terence have found more diverse roles:

> It involves so many different aspects of management, the personnel, the strategic planning, negotiating contracts with firms. There's always a change of scene, all this stimulating stuff as well the routine, suits me fine. (Edward)

> I run this office, sit on committees, run conferences for our members. We publish a lot. I edit our yearbook, deal with budgets, represent the organisation. I'm still involved in education. We have an educational resource centre here. I serve on two committees trying to establish new faith-based schools, and I'm a governor of my son's school. (Terence)

Terence has taken pleasure in the investment by his new organisation in technological support:

> School technology just didn't compare with the modern world. You were scrimping and scraping to get the minimum. Here you get what is right for the job. There's none of this: 'Oh where's the money going to come from?' attitude. Admin. staff are computer-literate. The quality just doesn't compare to schools. (Terence)

Edward has new opportunities for emotional learning and development:

> I'm learning a lot from my boss, partly from just watching her at work, partly from sessions where she gives me a lot of the background – what each person is like, how she's dealt with them, how I possibly should deal with them. I'm better at anticipating problems. Many people here have serious problems, inter-personal problems blown up out of all proportion, moments of illness, fitting. Sometimes they face you out, anger coming out of every pore, storming out, slamming doors, punching the wall. It frightens other people. It's quite intimidating. I've needed help from my boss to cope with this because of my inexperience. That's taken my skills in that line to the very limit. I need to get better at that but I'm learning fast. (Edward)

Edward, like Terence, finds himself in a situation where good management facilitates the honest expression of emotion:

> People here are very 'touchy-feely'. They respond to physical contact more because they often don't have the mental capacity to transmit feelings verbally. One of the nice things is that people express their feelings far more than so-called 'normal' situations. Their emotions are close to the surface, very child-like, but that's probably good. They're more human in some ways. They're very aware of each other's feelings. You'll see somebody giving someone else a cuddle because she's upset or he's upset. Quite often men break down in tears. Their emotions take over. They might fall into helpless fits of giggles. Their emotions are that bit bigger and stronger. It's much healthier they're out in the open. They're not as bound by the sort of conventions we are. (Edward)

> You get people very stressed, just lost somebody, and we're here. You're bound to get stressed situations in any organisation, but it can be contained. If somebody wants a moan, they'll have a moan and, good, let them off-load. You're not constrained by the organisation. (Terence)

Terence and Edward now experience less pressure and more flexibility. Both have protected time off within the working day:

> In schools you're more structured. You can't put children into a filing cabinet. You've got to be at lessons at particular times. I have a degree of flexibility. I can take my lunch when I want. I was on duty five days a week in school through lunchtime. It wasn't questioned. Because of that, I insist all staff here take their hour's lunch. They deserve it. (Terence)

Some of the group have achieved a new work/life balance:

> My job is a priority to me. My family is a priority to me. The two of them work well together whereas they didn't in school. I have more time with my family. There's a better quality, a new enthusiasm that I can devote, whereas in the past I might have been there in body but my mind was completely spaced out somewhere. (Terence)

They use their leisure time positively:

> Weekends are free. I can now do the conservation voluntary work I love. I'm much more of an asset at home now. I can now be more supportive. Work shouldn't occupy every waking moment and every sleeping moment. I go home with a song and a whistle. (Edward)

As in Zaccaro *et al* (1995), some of our teachers found organisations with a higher congruency between levels of self-efficacy and collective efficacy promoted self-renewal, emotional enrichment, continued feelings of success and greater self-esteem. Their experiences show that it is possible to find 'more exciting life spaces' after burnout but that this is highly dependent on the quality of life that is offered in the subsequent institutions. Individual and collective emotional capital can be enhanced through transactions that take place in positive emotional climates and this in turn facilitates the development of higher levels of emotional literacy. If schools were able to combine all the elements discussed above, they would generate the opportunity for high levels of emotional literacy and be more likely to generate the 'Healthy Schools, Healthy Teachers' ideal currently promoted by government (www.wiredforhealth.gov.uk).

Salaried work was not the only way the teachers reconstructed their identity. In particular those whose working lives did not fulfil their needs, like Alex and Margot, sought opportunities to reinvent themselves in more personal ways.

Reinventing the Self

> When cocoons fulfill their functions, butterflies emerge. (Hudson, 1991: 107)

For many of our teachers, new ways of being facilitated their self-growth. Self-renewal processes were viewed as empowering. Maureen, for example, felt

> ... it tempers you, ultimately makes you a very much stronger person. The riches that are achieved far outweigh any monetary loss. My pension may not be much, but I've got peace of mind now.

Hudson (1991: 96) maintains that life transitions proceed 'gradually and sporadically', typically taking up to three years. 'Grieving, healing, and renewal are organic and take time. There is no shortcut, no quick fix'. For Margot, self-renewal 'took an incredible amount of time' and Maureen also found that rebuilding her self-esteem took 'much, much longer than I expected, to come to terms with things'. Fifteen months later she was feeling 'very optimistic now, sparkling again'. Marcus, Margot and Emily talked of 're-birthing', the 'inner re-birth of self-esteem, vitality, and sufficiency' (Hudson, 1991: 112). Andrew felt his re-birthing was

> ... more external than internal. I've got into a different environment so things around me have changed and that's had an effect on me. Five years ago, I was very confident. I'm going back to what I was.

Not all our teachers could identify with the re-birthing concept. Alex, for example, is still feeling 'pretty down' six years later despite his 'return to a focus, a principled approach and direction' in life. But a number of our teachers were able to reinvent themselves to varying extents through their quest for spiritual fulfilment, their search for knowledge and understanding, and their increased levels of personal and social emotional literacy.

Spiritual fulfilment

As Margolis (1998) has described, new ways of being arose that stemmed from spiritual needs rather than those of a workplace dominated by work ethics and the self-interested rational self of modernity. Some of our teachers sought a deep spiritual identity, a return to the authentic self, where 'the purpose of life is joy' (Kitchens, 1994: 19), gained through listening to the inner voice, following the heart and finding 'flow', total immersion in valued activities. Fostering spirituality involves a 'disengagement' from 'false values' imposed by parents, organisations, community and society, a turning to 'true values, and acting consistently with these true values' and a redefining of 'moral and ethical positions and responsibilities' (Bergquist *et al*, 1993: 181). For Maureen, spirituality encompasses

> ... beauty, in a landscape, in a person, in shared experiences with the right person. The spiritual element of living is very important, recognising magic moments, the beauty in the world. Even if you don't recognise God as being the all-important being in your life, there must be time for something in everybody's life that feels absolutely wonderful. People live so very busy lives that they miss out.

Maureen prays 'anywhere and everywhere, thanking God for things beautiful'. Margot, 'a strong religious person', was 'looking for a new path, to be taken to God in a new direction. It did change me. I was seeking a new way of working'. Gareth too

> ... spent time with God, with His word. God was speaking so clearly and so forcefully into my life. 'Gareth, this is what I want you to do'. I

> was beginning to get buzzing again. I had such an assurance from God of His enabling and equipping me that it was bubbling up within me ... I knew that God had given me not only an impartation of ideas and vision that the church was lacking, but also an impartation of the ability to give this to other people. I want new birth within the church and that's very exciting.

Nurturing the self was reclaimed. Margot 'started to meditate. Reiki massage was heaven, utter heaven. I've never felt so pampered, so in control of my own spirit'. Some of our teachers created personal stability zones, internal and external sanctuaries. Important spiritual locations, 'my soul places' (Maureen), to be visited in person, and 'scenes fixed in the mind' (Maureen) fed inspiration. Special sites, such as the Avebury stone circle, 'helped enormously, enormous healing goes on there. Ancient places are so steeped in it' (Margot).

Creativity aided their spiritual renewal by enhancing their generativity and so regaining

> ... the artistic personality. I am not Pavlov's dog, always living to someone else's structure. I'm becoming the person I always thought I was, again. Being creative is how spirituality comes out in my life. (Maureen)

Luke is 'back to music again, composing, performing, African drumming. I'm completely free to do it. Even in my sleep I'm writing lyrics'. He has accepted his creative self, which he believes was 'outlawed' as contrary to childhood masculinity. 'I know where I want to be. I'm open to exploring ideas rather than trying to close them off'. Margot's paintings on the religious theme of standing stones are selling well. Alex plays in a semi-professional band and derives spiritual fulfilment from his creation of an internet site which provides free support materials for examination students. He is committed to access to knowledge being free, and by sharing information and ideas more 'in accord with my politics' he gains great satisfaction from the responses of his global students who range from Australia to Mexico, St. Vincent to Hong Kong.

Home surroundings also enhanced the spiritual self. Rachel and her husband reconstructed their farmhouse and converted one of their barns into an art studio. She felt 'a physical need to create, to express my feelings about the environment through doing a wall-hanging associated with the countryside and farming', so she created a small-holding. Her new home is 'really beautiful. It's got an intensity, a mystical spirituality, that did not exist in the city. I realise how much I love this place and how much I missed out by living in the city'. Charlotte, Margot and Maureen each created personal spiritual spaces that reflect their own spiritual needs, Margot and Charlotte using stones and sculptures in their gardens, while Maureen gave a 1950s look to her home and set up an art studio.

Some of our teachers understood how the values of their cultural inheritance had stunted their emotional literacy.

> Some of the things I'd been taught in the past by my mother, the work ethos, this 'You cannot allow people to help you. You've got to be in command'. All of that seemed such nonsense all of a sudden. Why can't I allow people to help me? There was something more to me that needed deeper respect from me. I had allowed people to take so much from me but I hadn't allowed anybody to put things back. My family were marvellous at putting it back. (Margot)

The teachers' perceptions of themselves had generally changed. They saw the self more in terms of connections to others – their family, friends or students. For example, Alex made contact with relatives he had not seen in adulthood and he deliberately chose his new post to be near like-minded childhood friends. Rachel found a group of like-minded musicians and artists, and has become involved in church activities, returning to her roots in youth work by helping to build a youth club. They focused on human emotions; their primary purpose was to develop human potential. They sought to enable themselves and those in their care to become physically, mentally and emotionally comfortable, Maureen's life, for example, became 'very much bound up with home making, making people feel happy and content, helping to make life more pleasurable'.

Knowledge and understanding

The re-birthing processes involved acquiring more sociological and psychological understanding, and amassing 'more self-knowledge' (Rebecca). Luke now acknowledges and utilises different parts of the self:

> I wasn't accepting who I was. It was finding parts of my nature I hadn't recognised before, lots of different aspects to me. Part of finding yourself is realising those aspects of your personality are you. You can

live with them, try to make the most of what they give you, rather than fighting against them.

Andrew learned

> ... how delicate a person's being can be. The way one feels inside is very, very dependent on how others are treating you and my own response to that. A person is actually formed by other people's perceptions of them. It's a two-way process. Sometimes what people say can reinforce what you think you know. So if you think you're not very good or failing, and someone says something that appears to reinforce that, it makes it worse. Whereas if you think you're succeeding, then conversely, any slight praise makes you feel much better, and any slight criticism you think: 'So what!' It depends on how vulnerable you are at the time, and what feedback you're getting. I wouldn't have thought before that other people could have had such an effect on my own belief in myself.

Most of them thought that the stress experience had been 'beneficial. It did force me to learn some hard lessons about myself which I wouldn't otherwise have learned' (Celia). 'It's taught me how to switch off, how to be calm, how to feel comfortable, to learn how to deal with stresses' (Luke). Alex talked of 'accepting [his] humanity, [his] historical weaknesses'. Marcus said 'that the quality of life is more important than a job or money'. They developed insight. Celia, like Charlotte, realised that part of the problem was

> ... I was selling my old teacher self, the one that I didn't really want to be any more, just to get a job, the one that conforms and dresses smartly in a suit! The power dressing woman, the controlling self, because I thought that was what they wanted. I wouldn't do that now. What I need is to feel like a free spirit ... I do need time to myself, for quiet and reflection.

Celia, Maureen and Ralph had acquired greater understanding of the conflict over assigned teacher identities:

> I was trained to work in a very kind of creative way. I've always been the sort of teacher kids like, always been popular, but always had a lot of conflict that hasn't been expressed, with management, because I don't do the expected thing. I had to leave teaching in the end, because my way of doing doesn't fit with what's wanted these days. My style isn't to be one of these ogre-ish kind of teachers. I don't want to be like that. I was repelled by the whole of the game. (Celia)

After their experiences, the teachers had a different conception of stress which included 'recognising the collective element in stress' (Maureen).

> Your body becomes ill because of stress, a counteraction thing to stop me doing things. You know you must stop and take stock. I stay off immediately. I haven't let students down at all. I don't feel guilty whereas before I would have. I'd have been worried. (Margot)

Some found it helpful to separate the spheres they operated in. Margot walks out of school

> ... at 3.30. I'm still conscientious but I'm not the way I was. I don't want anything to inflict school on this life. It upsets Stuart. It's a deliberate policy never to talk about work at home. (Margot)

Luke doesn't

> ... do any music in school. I prefer to keep it separate. I'm prepared to stay in school to finish my work, but then I'm always out, digging the garden, doing something outside. That's got to be *my* time.

They focused on fewer priorities but rated these more highly. Margot 'gave up all my jobs outside school. To have the courage to do that was terribly brave. I had to put the church work I was doing on hold. It took a lot of doing to say no to people in the village'.

It was clear that some of the teachers had learned what they could control and what was outside their control. 'It's shown me that no-one can control everything. There are some things beyond your control no matter how hard you struggle' (Rebecca). 'I know now that shit does happen. Life is far from ideal, so I had better accept that and get on with it' (Alex)

Individual emotional literacy

Some of our teachers had realised that emotional skills can be learned and that the needs of work today require these skills to be highly developed, both in order to be effective in social transactions and to facilitate emotional learning in others. 'Emotional mastery' involves identifying true feelings, acknowledging and appreciating emotions, knowing how they support people, and having curiosity about their signals and confidence in handling current and future emotions (Robbins, 1992).

Luke, Margot, Alex, Celia and Edward actively pursued the acquisition of emotional skills, so improving their own emotional resilience. They believed this would protect them against further stress-related illness, particularly by improving their own self-awareness, and would also be instrumental in helping them build collective adaptational resources and coping strategies with their colleagues. Alex acknowledged his failure to have 'developed the skills' to aid greater 'professional detachment' and become a 'shaper' of policy. Now he hoped to create 'manageable situations' through learning how to help people at 'grass roots level' solve their problems by 'empathising' without 'taking on board their personal baggage'. Feeling the need for 'creative teams, effective leadership, good human relations, innovations in professional development to seek quality improvement and challenge cynicism', he enhanced his professional practice by training as a counsellor in his own time, completing a PhD and an Advanced Certificate in Education Management so that he can contribute to quality improvement by helping build a positive emotional climate:

> It's made me listen more effectively. Before I started it, if I talked to colleagues, I approached it in the wrong way. I've learned different ways to approach things. I want to help people at work. I'm a problem-solver. I won't survive if I try to problem-solve everyone's problems. I've got to move into counselling mode to be more effective, for my own sanity as well as doing the job. Help them to identify problems and solve them.

Edward completed a management studies course in a local college. It was a 'social experience' that also allowed him to 'see ways in which I didn't manage very well'.

Some people found it easier than others to name and discuss emotions and emotional states. Celia, now a music therapist in a children's hospice, is part of a team in a culture where sharing emotional experiences and experiencing clinical supervision (Holloway, 1995) is the norm. Life there is highly emotional but, because of high levels of emotional literacy, emotion 'never gets out of control'. Like Andrew, Luke now shares his emotions with his partner. 'That's a rejuvenation process in itself, just talking about emotions' (Luke). Levels of emotional awareness increased. 'The plus is I'm more aware of what I need rather than what's expected of me' (Luke). Margot can now 'identify stress. If I get tired or stressed I lose my temper quickly. That's the sign for me that I've got to back off, think what I'm doing'. Although they still felt vulnerable, especially at times when feelings of depression hit them, some of our teachers now recognised these emotions for what they were, understanding that they were not permanent. Despite 'days when I still feel really, really, down' (Maureen), they knew these would pass. 'Good days will follow' (Maureen). 'Shit happens, and things cannot get worse than they have been' (Alex). They questioned what feelings of anxiety meant and whether they were justified. Furthermore, they were able to develop anticipatory strategies to deal with prospective anxiety, such as rehearsing responses to challenging encounters.

Emotion became an important signal to the self, enhancing their insight. Luke recognised his emotional distress sooner.

> I can see where my handwriting changes. Different styles tell me quite a lot about myself. It's the emotion of *how* you're writing things.... It's a battle because emotions make me scared. It's when the anxious becomes debilitating, that's the problem. Now I deal with them. I don't fight them. I don't put them away. I explore them and take time to do that. Make it more understandable.

Many of them found it easier to manage their emotions. 'I'm better than I was, much calmer. I've stopped smoking' (Margot). Meditation was a common resource. 'I want to concentrate on what I want to do. Through meditation I can get answers to what I want to do' (Margot).

> I let my mind drift off. It lets the emotions, the feelings, out of my mind, lets me recognise them, which I can draw on immediately I'm back fully conscious again. When I've done that, I'm ready to move, deal with things that are making me anxious, not to put them away, but to be able to give myself the strength to cope. (Luke)

Confidence in change management grew as they became more adept at 'working out how to make my working conditions work *for* me' (Maureen). Andrew told us:

> Trying to rebuild my confidence was an uphill task. I knew there were things I could do. It was a gradual build-up, starting with non-teaching,

> just able to do a job, then doing a few days teaching and realising it wasn't all gloom and doom. I could cope with it, even though it wasn't my subject. I could cope with the children. I was able to use my initiative. They didn't have to keep telling me what to do, and it just got better and better. Then the same school appointed me as science co-ordinator. This school closes in two years, but I feel confident that I will get another job. There's plenty of work out there. I can't see me doing anything else until I retire. I look forward to returning to teaching older children – that's what I'm missing. I know I can do it. I won't have to go through that horror again.

Their empathy skills improved. Alex was now 'more empathic and less opinionated', Andrew 'can recognise stress in other people', while Celia

> ... can talk about things because I've thought things through. I'm reasonably self-aware. ... I'm less judgemental. I've got greater empathy with people, more understanding of the difficult experiences people can find themselves in. It gives you a greater understanding of people's problems in coping with life; it makes you more compassionate.

Margot feels 'so sorry for the hierarchy who have that 'twitchy' look, so overawed by work, they can't smile. It's quite frightening'. She can more easily deal with the 'huge amounts of disaffected staff having trouble' in her role as union representative 'because I've been through it myself'.

It was important to be able to 'give something back' (Luke). Rachel was 'raising money for Stress at Work'. Luke now contributes to facilitating a positive emotional climate within his school. His experiences have given him high levels of emotional literacy and this allows him 'to reciprocate', to create 'opportunities to help others' by making conscious efforts towards reducing the pressures on staff so as to de-intensify the requirements of the job. He recognises early signs of stress in his colleagues and students. He can empathise with them and share emotional experiences, showing others that their emotions are 'normal'. He actively campaigns for changes in policy to deal with stress and supports local authority initiatives. Nonetheless, he recognises when emotional labour becomes emotional toil:

> I don't want to become everyone's unloading host. I haven't time. That's going to make me ill as well. I now know when to stop doing that. I only give what I can. I don't give more than I can. I wouldn't have time for myself.

The teachers regarded their enhanced levels of emotional literacy as effective for managing stress. 'It wouldn't happen again. My perception of myself – that I was useless – was incorrect. I wasn't useless. If I was wrong then, then I'd probably be wrong again' (Andrew).

Most of out teachers recovered a sense of their essential self. 'I can be me' (Celia). 'If I don't have *my* time, then I'm not me and I'll lose me. I've got to recognise that who I am is important to my sanity' (Luke). The recovery was gradual. Twelve months later, the stressed teacher 'doesn't exist anymore' for Marcus. He is 'once again the person I'm used to being'. Andrew reports feeling: 'It's more like the real me'; Alex that: 'I'm getting emotionally stronger every day, more in control of my life, of what can hurt me now'. The stress experience proved empowering and ultimately enriching to several of our teachers. As Luke declared, 'gradually over the last five years I'm a better person for what I've been through'.

Teachers came to terms with their losses and regained their physical, mental and emotional agility. 'It was a slow downhill and it's been an equally slow climb back. Now I feel I'm at the summit and I can see for miles. I can see what was wrong before' (Andrew). They re-evaluated their lives and rebuilt their selves. Rebecca 'lost my job, and it's OK. I lost what I saw as a long-term career. I lost my sense of identity. I still survived it'. For some, the self was enhanced. Gareth declared, 'I'm so excited, so thrilled, so enjoying what I am doing'. Jessica's joyful commitment shines through: 'There's no way I want to leave this place. I'm here till they carry me out in a wooden box!'

Conclusion

The last three chapters show that the teachers in the study, all clinically diagnosed as undergoing stress, went through an identity passage and what this process entailed. We have argued that stress is not simply a physical, mental or psychological condition but a process wherein the individual undergoes change. During stress, personal identities come under attack, perhaps through the introduction of new required social identities. If these are in sharp conflict with the person's self-concept, key elements of the self are stripped away until one is outside the pale of society. Losing social referents leads to losing sight of who we are. Once this takes hold in the workplace, stress can spread like a virus into other inter-connected social areas, like families, eating still further into their personal identity. Teachers' ontological security becomes marred, producing cognitive and emotive dissonance (Giddens, 1991; Hochschild, 1979). What a 'good teacher' should now be, how 'good' teachers should now think, feel, and act, did not concur with our teachers' beliefs about their own behaviour, thinking and feeling. They lost confidence in their own teaching capabilities. Biographical disruption (Williams, 2000) ensued. Their conviction that they were no longer 'good' teachers fed feelings of loss, anxiety and depression. They were plunged into a downward spiral, marked by deeply negative emotions.

The plunge into despair does not go on forever, however, and chapter 4 describes the period of transition, in which the teachers 'bottom out', followed by a 'cocooning' process in which they take time and space for the reflexive self to engage in 'identity work'. Signs are noted of the beginnings of re-engagement with society and reconstruction of the self, and the value of assistance from significant others. Chapter 5 reports on the results of re-engagement which, in some cases but not all, developed into full-scale self-renewal.

It will be seen that self-renewal for those who experienced it involved the recovery of identity losses suffered during the downward spiral recounted in chapter 3. These people had acquired new emotional skills and literacy, new knowledge and understanding, greater control and autonomy, and they were once again enjoying positive emotional experiences. In short, there was closer consonance between the assigned social identity attached to the position they now held and their self-concept, and more amenable social contexts for the resultant personal identity to flourish. The interaction between the two – self and context – is important. Context is not an absolutely immovable constraint and can be seen and experienced in different ways. What has been gained is this flexibility of view in the reassertion of agency.

This journey was an emotional one for everybody. Extreme and traumatic emotions were experienced, emotions that were not just a matter of psychic or physical release but which were socially structured by prevailing conditions and policies that demanded a change in identity. This is consistent with other research we have conducted in recent years (Jeffrey and Woods, 1996, Troman and Woods, 2001). The traumas of 'separation' were induced in the first place by the new performativity, rational-technocratic discourse of schooling. But, as we have shown here, they were then taken over by the impulsions of the identity passage. We can see identity as 'almost social roles in movement, located in particular subject positions .... Affirmed, denied, renegotiated or redefined over time and in relation to others', functioning as both 'a way of understanding and a politics of resistance' (Clark *et al*, 1996: 72/73).

We can see, too, how some selves became fragmented, and there is evidence that this is happening elsewhere among educationists. Beatty (1999: 19) speaks of the 'fragmentation of the teacher's professional self' in response to certain systemic changes in Canada. Woods and Jeffrey (2002) found English primary teachers whose identity had been isomorphic (Nias, 1989) were separating their working and personal lives, as did some of the teachers in this sample. At the same time, however, we can see how some teachers have reassembled their identities around an esteemed notion of self. To be sure, only three of our sample engaged with the new social identity of the professional teacher in the school where their stress had built up. The rest found salvation by either changing their work context and/or modifying their role and commitment, or moving outside the teacher social identity altogether. Whatever the outcomes, active processes of reflexive self-identity are at work in every instance. Recovery processes are not closed off by the fragmentation of experience. There is evidence of much powerlessness in the separation phase, but signs of re-empowerment are clearly visible in the self-renewal phase.

6

Implications for Education

The account and analysis of teacher stress as presented in this book have profound implications for education. As well as the trauma experienced by the individual teacher, there is also enormous wastage to the educational system. Our teachers are the tip of the iceberg – their experience is far from unique. There are many stressed teachers who have not been clinically diagnosed. There are many teachers who have not yet come to terms with their new social identity. A great deal of emotional energy is being wasted. Many identities are on the defensive, on the verge of, or in the throes of, the downward spiral. It is not surprising that the country has a massive problem over teacher supply and retention. It is clear that policy changes that will reflect the affective needs of teachers and their students are sorely needed. As Blackmore (1996) points out, the emotional landscapes of teaching are shaped not only by individuals but also by social, political and institutional forces. Teacher stress is a public issue; it is socially generated within relational and organisational processes. The educational system together with the school and individual are therefore foci for intervention. We discuss each, not forgetting that it is the complex interaction among them that produces such damaging levels of stress.

There is much excellent advice available on avoiding stress, from organisations and agencies like the Health Education Authority (1988), the NUT (1990); the Education Service Advisory Committee (1998); and from writers and researchers who have studied teacher stress, such as Mills (1990 and 1995), Dunham (1992) and Kyriacou (2000). Troman and Woods (2001) offer a chapter of recommendations. We complement the advice offered in these resources with some recommendations arising directly from this study of emotionality as it affects teachers.

Educational system level

> 'It needs society-wide recommendations, not just school recommendations'. (Luke)
>
> 'The biggest shift that could be made (to alleviate teacher stress) would be one that involved moving from a competitive, marketing, managerialist discourse to a more co-operative, humanist, democratic one'. (Troman and Woods, 2001: 146)

We argue that stress is not simply an issue of personal vulnerabilities, nor of organisational aspects but that it is caused by 'ecological dysfunction' (Hopkins, 1997) brought about by a combination of personal, organisational and societal factors. Societal factors are fundamental. Because stress is a complex and multi-level phenomenon, it is difficult to show causation. It can hardly be a coincidence, however, that the escalation of stress levels cited in our introduction to this book has corresponded with a spate of government reforms designed to restructure and reculture the education system. These reforms were underwritten by a discourse totally at variance with that espoused by many teachers and central to their teaching practice and personal identities. The differences were starkly revealed at times of the early Ofsted inspections, which engendered a great deal of stress among teachers. We quote one research study on the effects of Ofsted inspections in primary schools, which sought to explain the strong, disruptive feelings aroused among the teachers. Jeffrey and Woods (1998) set out the values differences like this:

A. Knowledge

Ofsted Values	**Teacher Values**
Prescribed National Curriculum	Negotiated National Curriculum
Controlled National Curriculum	Flexible and autonomous practices
Emphasis on products	Emphasis on process
Subject-based curriculum	Child-centred, holistic, integrative
Systematization, standardization	Differences, diversity
Uniformity	

B. Pedagogy

Ofsted Values	Teacher Values
Transmissional	Creative
Behaviourist	Constructivist learning theory
Formal	Informal contexts
Examination	Support
Instant performance	Learning takes time

C. Assessment (of pupils and teachers)

Ofsted Values	Teacher Values
Formal	Informal
Quantitative	Qualitative
Standardized	Localized
Periodic tests	Continuous
Hierarchical examination	Collective engagement, self-assessment
Simplicity	Complexity

D Culture

Ofsted Values	Teacher Values
Competition	Collegiality
Blame	Support
Managerialism	Professionalism
Control	Self-regulation
Consumer	Producer

(Jeffrey and Woods, 1998: 82-3)

The researchers argued that

> ... there is a basic clash of values here. And it is a conflict where teachers are in the weaker position. They are under examination in a disciplinary exercise, where their humanistic morality has been replaced by one centred on rational-technicism. We have seen a number of comments here about teachers feeling that they were losing control of their own classrooms, and their very selves. (*ibid*: 83-4)

The chart above demonstrates the gulf between government policy and teacher values. Though derived from Ofsted inspections in primary schools, it is equally applicable to secondary schools – this book has abundantly illustrated most of these features and the consequences of the clash between the two discourses. Government policy has placed emphasis on 'performativity' (Ball, 1998; Broadfoot, 1998), an ideology of 'performance' which has fixed goals, task analysis and testing, and which excludes any alternative view. There has been much more prescription over teaching, and less independent professional judgement. Values of care and creativity have been squeezed out in the new instrumentalism and the all-consuming drive for 'higher standards' as measured by objective tests. Managerialism has replaced collegiality. 'Heavy-duty accountability' (Woods and Jeffrey, 1996: 43) has replaced professionalism and trust. The values of the market, with schools in competition for students and for resources, epitomised in annual 'league tables', have come to prevail. Teachers' work has intensified during the 1990s (Hargreaves, 1994), as all their spare moments at school and much of their home lives has become taken over by lesson preparation, form-filling, reports and just battling to keep up with the pace of change.

There can be little doubt that the Government – Conservative in the 1980s and early 1990s, New Labour since 1997 – has to bear much of the responsibility for the dramatic increase in teacher stress. Moreover, it seems likely that this was known and considered to be a price worth paying (ie for 'higher standards'). Nothing was to deflect the government from its task – or its methods. Teachers were held responsible for the alleged national decline, particularly because of their devotion to 'progressive teaching methods'. In the early 1990s, they were subjected to a 'discourse of derision' in the national media (Ball, 1990; Wallace, 1993), as the government set about a 'return to basics'. Newspaper headlines proclaimed: 'The Plowden party is finally over', and 'Education's insane bandwagon goes into the ditch' (quoted in Woods and Wenham, 1995: 131). Teacher status and morale has never recovered.

At bottom, this has a great deal to do with the growth of distrust in the society of late modernity. The 'debilitating effects of modern institutions on self-experience and the emotions' gain ascendency through the absence or fracturing of trust (Giddens, 1990: 100). The absence of trust leads to rising anxiety, which

> ... tends to threaten awareness of self-identity, since awareness of the self in relation to constituting features of the object-world becomes obscured. It is only in terms of the basic security system, the origin of the sense of ontological security, that the individual has the experience of self in relation to a world of persons and objects organised cognitively through basic trust. (Giddens, 1991: 45)

This is how global trends penetrate to the core of the self: via government policy, hierarchical institutional management and heavy-duty surveillance.

This is not to say that the educational reforms have been wholly without benefit. The idea of a National Curriculum is now widely accepted as a basic entitlement for students and a framework for teachers. Coverage and teaching in some areas, such as science, has been much improved. There has been en- and re-skilling for teachers as well as de-skilling (Campbell and Neill, 1994; Osborn 1995; Cooper and McIntyre, 1996). There has been an improvement in standards as measured by tests. The problem seems to lie in degree and balance. How can the best results of the reforms be maintained while the worst are modified to allow more of the humanitarian discourse, represented in the teacher values in the table above, back into the reckoning, and hence more improvement, more rounded education, more moral discourse? How can the best of the humanitarian, welfarist discourse of the 1970s (Gewirtz and Ball, 2000) be retained while allowing for some rational systematisation? Does it have to be one or the other? We have pursued a policy of extremes over the last fifty years, swinging from 'traditionalism' to 'progressivism' and back again to yet more robust and exclusive traditionalism. We need a shift back into equilibrium between educational improvement and teachers' functionality and well-being – the two are indissolubly connected.

There have been signs in government recently of a growing awareness of some of these problems. A 1998 Green Paper seemed to signal a new age:

> The present arrangements reflect a different era. We need a new vision of a profession which offers better rewards and support in return for higher standards. Our aim is to strengthen school leadership, provide incentives for excellence, engender a strong culture of professional development, offer better support to teachers to focus on teaching in the classroom, and improve the image, morale and status of the profession. (DfEE, 1998)

The Government set up a committee in 1999 to report on 'creative and cultural education' (NACCCE, 1999), and welcomed its findings, promising more flexibility and creativity in the next curriculum revision (DfEE, 1999). A recent Green Paper (DfEE, 2001) stated:

> We will demonstrate trust in the informed professional judgement of teachers while maintaining a focus on accountability and standards (p.8)

It talks about partnerships, greater autonomy and freedom for successful schools, reducing the bureaucratic burden on teachers, increasing the investment in ICT, creating new rewarding career paths.

In a pamphlet accompanying a speech to the Social Market Foundation entitled *Professionalism and Trust – the future of teachers and teaching* (November 2001), the Secretary of State for Education and Skills, Estelle Morris, signalled 'a new era of trust in our professionals on the part of Government', noting that no reform would work without the dedication of high quality staff. Teachers, she said, are 'a national asset of priceless value. But as a nation we have not always treated them as such' (p.1). They need time and support to do their work.

> We want to free the energies, talents and creativity of heads, governors and teachers to support them to achieve higher standards and to enable them to innovate and move towards earned autonomy. (*ibid.* p.6)

In considering the vexed question of teacher supply and retention, currently a major issue, Morris recognises that 'the teacher morale and workload issues...have a negative impact not only on the desire of some serving teachers to remain in teaching but also on deterring others from joining the profession' (p.13). Her vision of the future includes teachers enjoying more 'status and responsibility, and a better work/life balance' (p.14). They will have more resources, more time for planning and thinking, and will be supported by a range of other adults in the school, high quality facilities and modern ICT. She compares teachers with doctors in relation to professional development. In the future, 'More teachers [will] say 'I enjoy my job'. Fewer teachers are leaving the profession for the wrong reasons. More are coming back for the right ones' (p.18). Towards the end of her speech, she declares:

> There is no doubt that Governments over the last 30 years have not always rushed to express their confidence in teachers. But we are leaving those days behind and entering a new and positive era. (p.26)

While the accountability measures of performativity are here to stay, 'teachers have earned the trust of all of us and we give it willingly' (*ibid.*).

The speech borrows from both the discourses in the table above. This is surely what the magic, hitherto unattainable balance would look like. But is it achievable in practice? Has the Government a clear enough vision of what education is for, and how to achieve it, and does this vision show an equally balanced discourse? (see Fielding, 2001). In reply, the Education Secretary could point to the independent study by Price Waterhouse Coopers (PwC) she commissioned of teacher workloads in 2001. This has been referred to the School Teacher's Review Body (STRB) for advice on its recommendations, expected in the Spring of 2002. In its final report (December 2001), PwC identify all the issues which have been explored at length in this book, including the fact that

- teachers work more intensive weeks than other comparable professionals
- teachers perceive a lack of control and ownership over their work
- while welcoming the spirit of many reforms, teachers found the pace and manner of change burdensome and counter-productive
- teachers were insufficiently supported to meet the changes
- teachers were not accorded the professional trust they merited

PwC conclude:

> Within the context of DfES' national programme to transform the school workforce and secondary education, we therefore believe an essential strand will be to reduce teacher workload, foster increased teacher ownership, and create the capacity for managing change in a sustainable way that can lay the foundation for improved school and pupil perfomance in the future.

PwC presents a comprehensive programme to achieve these aims, and this is now under consideration. The burden of the report is to indicate that, given the will, such changes are achievable. The magic recipe of combined discourses is possible. Government documents since its publication have clearly been influenced by the report (for example, the Green Paper on extending opportunities and raising standards for 14 to 19 year olds, DfES, 2002b; the pamphlet on *Education and Skills: Delivering Results. A Strategy to 2006*, DfES, 2002c) and for the first time teacher unions and local government employers have combined to make a joint submission to the School Teachers' Review Body to limit the excessive workload of teachers, wanting a limit to the current open-ended demands on their time; a maximum number of teaching hours; a defined time for professional duties such as marking and preparation; and limits on duties relating to teaching and management (reported in *Education*, No, 46, 1 March 2002).

The discussion here centres on the very heart and soul of what education is and how it is to be delivered and organised. Teacher stress cannot be separated from that. In terms of the central theme of this book, a recognition of the significance of feelings and emotions in teaching and learning has at last penetrated policy-makers' thinking, challenging the current instrumentalism. The affective side of teaching is the currency of the teachers' discourse in the table above, and it is this which has to be restored to a significant degree. Education is not, nor never can be, a rational-calculative matter. There needs to be more cognisance of positive emotions that boost teaching and learning and of the negative emotions that impede and counter it. There are considerable implications for educational policy, for teacher training, and for teacher inservice development. It is encouraging that this is beginning to be recognised in government reports and statements. It remains to be seen whether this is political rhetoric or a real basis for action.

Institutional level

This book has noted evidence of school failings – lack of support structures, inflexibility, negative emotional climates, bullying hierarchical management, autocratic decision-making, poor communication systems, disregard of work/life issues. However, even in this rational-technocratic era, schools do not have to operate that way. Schools can address stress-related issues by interceding at three levels:

- Primary intervention: '*preventive* action to reduce or eliminate stressors (i.e. sources of stress) and with positively promoting a supportive and healthy work environment'
- Secondary intervention: 'concerned with the *prompt detection and management* of depression and anxiety by increasing self-awareness and improving stress management skills'
- Tertiary intervention 'concerned with the *rehabilitation* and *recovery process* of those individuals who have suffered or are suffering from ill-health as a result of stress'. (Earnshaw and Cooper, 1996: 98-99, their italics)

a) Primary level – preventive

All schools have a legal duty of care towards their employees regarding psychiatric injury (Health and Safety at Work Act (HASAWA) 1974; Management of Health and Safety at Work Regulations (MHSW) 1992; Rogers and Rayment, 1995), and must treat stress 'like any other health hazard ... keeping an eye out for developing problems and being prepared to act' (HSE, 1995:8).

First, schools must ensure 'health is not placed at risk through excessive and sustained levels of stress arising from the way work is organised, the way people deal with each other at their work or from the day-to-day demands placed on their workplace' (*ibid*). They must make themselves more aware of how the nature of the workplace creates sources of stress, such as excessive workloads and the long hours culture, and how these may be affecting their own organisation; they must assess the risks to the mental health of teachers (and of others who may be affected by the school's activities); they must make arrangements for putting into practice the preventive and protective measures required and carry out, where appropriate, a health surveillance; and they must give adequate information and training about risks to health (Earnshaw and Cooper, 1996: 53).

Despite extensive and decades-long research into stress and burnout, the high profile given to stress and stress-related illness, and increasing professional advice for employers on avoiding accusations of causing employee injury, interventions are 'comparatively rare' at primary level (Earnshaw and Cooper, 1996: 99). Few employers tackle these issues with sufficient rigour (Shillaker, 1997). Not one of our teachers reported their school taking stress seriously when adhering to health and safety regulations. None of the schools involved had formal stress management policies. The teachers' narratives portrayed schools as being slow to follow the lead of industry in protecting employees through formal employee assistance programmes (EAPs) or performance of stress audits. Risk assessments were not observed.

There was little evidence of preventive and protective measures to increase awareness and monitor and manage stress. At most, leaflets on stress were placed in pigeon-holes (Charlotte) or pay-slips (Stephen). 'The pro-active management of stress, which is supposed to be there, an authority-wide programme, is not being implemented, not enough resources, not enough people' (Ralph). Information and training must be freely available. Teachers need to feel safe if they question the levels of provision. Every school needs individual teachers with high levels of emotional literacy, who have the skills to assess risks and scrutinise stress levels and instigate and maintain quality improvement. Local authority agencies provide opportunities to develop skills in stress auditing, health surveillance, preventive and protective measures, information and training about risks.

Still at primary level, there needs to be greater acknowledgement that particular organisational cultures encourage the development of environments, policies and behaviours to be either supportive or abusive. Our teachers' identities have to be seen within the context of the emotional climates of their schools. In all cases these emotional climates were negative, characterised by fear, mistrust, blame, lack of respect and chronic anxiety, which inspired low levels of individual and collective emotional competences, and increased emotional labour. Schools need to promote caring organisational values and behaviours that prevent the occurrence of victimisation, harassment and bullying from occurring, and that actively mobilise positive emotional experiences, thus improving the affective health of employees.

One way of creating a healthier workplace is to implement principles and techniques derived from total quality management (TQM), which directs action to the process of work rather than the workers (Taylor and Hill, 1993). TQM is a 'participative, systematic approach to planning and implementing a continuous organisational improvement process' (Kaluzny *et al*, 1992). It can be a useful tool in reducing the number and quality of stressors. It promotes a listening culture, where stress is openly and safely acknowledged without fears of stigma, failure or threats to personal competence, where errors are accepted as part of the organisational learning process, where time is provided for problem solving, and where trust, reciprocal confidentiality, dignity, honesty, care, decency, passion, warmth, fun, challenge and excitement all contribute to the creation of positive emotional climates (Henry, 1994). The American state of Georgia, for example, successfully implemented TQM as a 'reform vehicle' and their bottom-up approach eliminated much of the distress in their schools (Weller and Hartley, 1994). The programmes offered in our teachers' schools, however, as in Walton Green, such as the Investors in People Initiative, are all too often 'sticking plaster' (Jonathon) that have been imposed from above:

> It is being used ineffectively, as a reward accreditation as opposed to something that is a *consequence* of the system improving. It's grafted on top. It should be a consequence not a starting point. (Alex)

To succeed requires a whole school approach in which teachers hold ownership of processes and are given sufficient time and resources to implement them.

Developing collaborative cultures based on participative decision-making with colleagues who have a common mission can reduce stress. Teachers at Walton Green considered the managerialistic styles of monitoring and appraisal as being too often concerned with surveillance and finding fault, rather than with rewarding success and fostering feelings of self-efficacy. The macho management styles so common in schools (Court, 1994) have been widely criticised for creating low trust corporate cultures that lower productivity (Helsby, 1999). According to Professor Gareth Jones of Henley Management College, cited in Coles (1997), such 'mercenary' cultures, obsessed as they are with measuring standards and outcomes and characterised by their narrow focus, task-orientation, external and internal competitiveness, poor co-operation and intolerance of poor performance and dissent, lead to negative emotional climates. Teachers need constructive feedback on their professional practice, recognition and praise. Good teaching requires emotional bonding. Teachers need time to develop satisfying emotional relationships with their students and colleagues. As Terence's experience shows, many work settings now adopt 'softer' management styles where 'people firms are happier firms' (Gomer, 1999: 1). The emphasis is on investing in staff, providing a range of services such as flexible benefits packages, career breaks, career advice, technological investment, time for reflection and learning opportunities.

Negative emotional climates are a consequence of the way government policy has been implemented, but this is not inevitable. Research on primary teachers' stress (Troman and Woods, 2001) identified a low-stress school, characterised by high levels of trust, open relationships, democratic participation (involving sharing values, knowledge and expertise, responsibilities, resources and humour), support for one another, emotional understanding (of self and others), and a pragmatic realism about policy implementation. Headteachers and senior management teams in low-stress schools play key roles in balancing the introduction of reform initiatives, organising and maintaining commitment to stress reduction policies.

The head of the King's school in Wolverhampton, which is part of the government's Fresh Start programme, Tim Gallagher (cited in Revell, 2000), argues that although good management cannot eliminate stress, it can create working conditions which reduce stress for staff. Among his first tasks at King's were: addressing the long hours' culture; introducing a 'no-blame', listening culture; reducing the climate of fear by giving all the staff job security; instituting regular staff development reviews which 'celebrate strengths and identify needs'; and accepting that stressed teachers need time to recover and time to ease back gradually into their jobs. The Well-Being Project in Norfolk (TBF, 2001) encourages schools to examine internal structures and relationships, and gives individuals the power to influence their working lives. Here, optimal performance is enhanced by creating enabling listening cultures of safety in the institutions.

The third primary approach deals with the way that, as Alex argued, much teacher stress is associated with insufficient skills and resources for dealing with human relations. Data from our sample suggest that teachers' health is put at risk by the high levels of emotional labouring demanded of them. The responsibility for emotional labour within schools fell mainly on the women teachers in our study, increasing their emotional toil. It was chiefly they who consumed most emotional capital in carrying out this 'unfair' burden (Margot) of coping with troubled students and troubled members of staff. Discussing the 'invisibility' (Charlotte) of much of the emotional transactions they were daily involved in, they observed that male teachers too often 'did not notice' (Rebecca) the distress surrounding them or chose to 'ignore' or 'avoid' it (Sally). Both Marcus and Andrew acknowledged that they avoided much of the emotional labouring with their students and colleagues.

The women recognised the value of this work, and keenly felt the loss of the time they needed to accomplish this with satisfaction, knowing that squeezing the time it required was detrimental to the students' quality of life. Whereas the women teachers felt emotional labouring tasks were part of their remit as teachers and colleagues, some of the men felt that these aspects were not their responsibility or that their skills were inadequate. Andrew and Marcus, for example, who had both come into teaching to 'teach [their] subject', felt they were now expected also to have the skills of a 'social worker' and they did not want to have to develop such skills. Ralph spoke of the 'feminisation of teaching', and the threat this posed for male teachers, who still expected female colleagues to perform the caring roles in school. The men in our study felt that the interpersonal skills demanded for collaborative teamworking and caring for large numbers of students who had EBD, both traditionally associated with women, were not within their grasp. Teachers who had to introduce new curriculum practices felt ill-equipped to deal with the emotional labour involved in managing teacher resistance. Jonathon was right to suggest that we would find that his co-ordinator's role, with its need for high levels of interpersonal skills, was a main factor in the creation of stress. Alex and Margot argue that in 2002, despite government initiatives such as the Healthy Schools programme (see www.wiredforhealth.gov.uk which provides 'health information for teachers') and the Healthy Workplace programme stemming from the green paper *Saving Lives: Our Healthier Nation* (DoH, 1999), many headteachers, deputy heads and departmental heads are 'dropping like flies' (Alex), still 'demoralised' by excessive workloads and excessive emotional labouring.

Emotional education for teachers and school management must be put higher on the political agenda. When curriculum delivery takes priority over student care, the time available for supporting students and colleagues is reduced. Teachers have less time to nurture, to explain, to increase pupils' emotional literacy and to increase their own emotional competences. Our teachers felt that the need to maintain pupil numbers and protect the school's reputation led to secrecy about the problems their school faced. They believed this compounded the schools' problems with instituting programmes designed to enable students to understand and regulate their destructive impulses, manage conflict, build emotional literacy and improve their behaviour. Dealing with disturbed children requires a full complement of emotional competences. Headteachers need high levels of emotional literacy and excellent skills in the emotions of leadership and human resource management.

Unlike in the spheres of commerce and industry, professional development and directed time was not forthcoming in schools for teachers to acquire and practise emotional skills. Alex, for instance, realised that his interpersonal skills were inadequate for managing the human resources in his department. Emotional competences can only be learned within co-operative relationships that eschew physically and psychologically destructive power plays, dishonesty and secrets (Steiner, 2000). Government initiatives to increase student attainment through improving literacy and numeracy may well be doomed to failure unless both students and teachers can develop good emotional literacy. Unless teachers are helped to enhance their own emotional competences, there is little chance of improving those of students. As Ros Bayley, an educational consultant cited in Phillips (1999) asserts, 'You can't foster in others what you don't have yourself. You have to start with the teachers and enable them to be emotionally literate'. Goleman, Cherniss and colleagues, for example, provide guidelines for 'best practice' and for 'securing organisational support for emotional intelligence efforts' on their website (www.eiconsortium.org).

b) Secondary level – detection and management

Good management is the key to identifying, understanding and managing stress at an early stage (Revell, 2000). This requires school management and the whole school population to increase their skills in emotional awareness and empathy. There would be fewer degradation ceremonies and less stigmatisation, and more chance of stress being headed off and normalised before the cascade took hold and plunged teachers to 'rock bottom'. If the site of conflict is identity, the organisation might take steps to facilitate accommodation to new measures without risk to its aims or to the individual's beliefs and values. There is still an 'implementation gap' (Ball and Bowe, 1992; Fitz, 1994) which allows schools a degree of negotiability in carrying out government policy.

The loss of reflective time contributed to stress developing; allowing for such time could stem and possibly even reverse the process. The escalation of stress-related illness can be prevented by creating a culture that gives teachers permission to be absent to make a full recovery, with appropriate practical backup provided in the classroom. Returning to school too soon hindered the analysis of underlying issues and this impaired the quality of social transactions in the workplace, resulting in physical and emotional overload, and, in many cases, precipitating complete emotional breakdown.

Our research indicates that some schools need to take their responsibilities for safeguarding the emotional health of teachers more seriously. All schools must take 'reasonable steps' to protect their staff from 'foreseeable harm' (Shillaker, 1997: 26). Our teachers' schools were aware of their difficulties and vulnerable health. Some teachers had presented medical certificates citing, for example, 'depression' (Charlotte, Rebecca, Andrew, Edward, William), 'depression and anxiety' (Stephen), 'neurasthenia' (Celia), 'stress' (Ralph). Terence was absent more frequently to attend the diabetic clinic. Sally had two weeks off after her father's death. Yet teachers who were suffering anxiety and depression were allowed back into classrooms – for reasons to do with the demands of budget requirements, curriculum needs and teacher shortages. Some reported that management structures and strategies added to their distress when they returned. Ralph, Margot, Alex, Andrew and Jonathon, for example, found their workloads increased on their return and they faced longer working days and restructured timetables for reasons of finance and school discipline.

The importance of social support systems in helping people to recover from stress-related illness and regain their well-being is well documented (Pines *et al*, 1981; Buyssen, 1996). Social support not only 'moderates the impact of stressors on well-being' but also influences 'the appraisal of environmental demands as stressful' (Griffith *et al*, 1999: 517). Our research suggests that our teachers' use of emotion-focused coping strategies was partly due to the emotional climate and organisational culture of their educational institution. Talking with trusted others is one key way of gaining insight and reappraising one's personal, collective and organisational meanings. But their individual and collective strategies precluded open discussion, which in turn inhibited the experience of emotionality and the recognition and understanding of their own feelings and the feelings of others. Consequently their levels of collective emotional awareness and empathy could not be adequately developed. Our data indicates, furthermore, that those who provide social support themselves risk increased emotional toil. Schools need highly skilled personnel who have directed time to perform the emotional labour required to deliver effective support. When our teachers' schools did provide some professional support, it was inadequate. As Lazarus (1990) notes, there is wide variation in people's perceptions of support, the ability to accept or use it, the skills and time of professionals, family members and friends, and there are differences between what is offered and what is received.

As we have seen, professional support may not necessarily be interpreted, or received, as a benefit, partly because it increases demands on time and workload, which for example, made Emily, 'iller'.

We have seen that teachers' stress impacts negatively on their performance. How schools respond to issues surrounding teacher competence reflects management's organisational emotional competence in handling relationships and conflict. Schools need to consider more fully how they approach so-called 'failing' teachers. Some of our teachers suffered additional emotional toil because of the threat of competency procedures. On their return to school, Stephen, Emily, Celia, Sally, William, Andrew and Terence reported suffering further harm from the emotional trauma caused by their school's interventions regarding their perceived competence to teach. The issue of teacher competence has maintained a high public profile since former chief inspector of schools Chris Woodhead asserted that there were 15,000 'failing' teachers (O'Reilly, 1999). The UK National Work-stress Network 5th annual conference report (2001) suggest that 'the inappropriate use of competency procedures' is a 'common tool to isolate weaker individuals'.

Some of our teachers perceived the threat of future competency proceedings as a political tool, used to intimidate them. Terence, Andrew, Sally and Celia, outspoken in their opposition to some consequences of educational reform, felt the threat of competency procedures was used to 'silence' them and remove troublesome organisational emotions. According to the Advisory, Conciliation and Arbitration Services (ACAS, 1977, ch.9), disciplinary procedures 'should not be viewed primarily as a means of imposing sanctions. They should be designed to emphasise and encourage improvements in individual conduct'. The teachers perceived the measures imposed not as rehabilitation but as punishment. The focus of inquiry tended to be task-oriented, so the improvement focus was also task-oriented, not person- or process-oriented, and sought no diagnosis of underlying problems. Past achievements and positive appraisals were disregarded. The label 'incompetent' was perceived as ensuring increased managerial scrutiny and the likelihood of fault being found more often with their work.

Schools need to make use of individual and collective emotion as a bonding agent and as a signal to indicate areas for quality improvement. As Blackmore (1996: 338) argues, 'the expression of emotion serves a communicative role in developing a sense of community, a tolerance of ambiguity, and greater understanding through empathy'. As a locus of resistance, emotion can point to areas where policy change needs to be addressed. As Jonathon and Alex pointed out, the adoption of individualised approaches in Walton Green discounted the value of emotion as a facilitator and indicator of thinking (Salovey and Sluyter, 1997) and reduced key organisational emotional competences, such as emotional awareness and empathy (Goleman, 1998), so inhibiting problem recognition and resolution. Schools must develop their emotional antennae. Emotions are communicative processes that provide information about personal and social identity claims to the self and to others (Parkinson, 1996). Negative emotions, inimical to teaching and learning, have a social meaning. High emotional states and trauma may signify individual and organisational turbulence caused by the strains and tensions within institutions. As Obholzer and Roberts (1994) maintain, 'troubled' individuals are bound to 'troubled' organisations. Teachers have to 'feel right' in order to teach to their optimum efficiency (Riseborough, 1981). Understanding their social referents rather than individualising and pathologising them might offset the worst educational consequences of teachers' stress. Understanding negative and positive emotion, and addressing the problems indicated by negative emotion is likely to be more fruitful for organisational health and for productivity than the disregard, repression or removal of emotionality.

c) Tertiary level – Rehabilitation

One key problem of rehabilitation is determining whether the stress was caused chiefly by conditions at home or at work, and therefore who has responsibility for recovery processes. Following the John Walker case in 1996, the law decreed that organisations are responsible only for treating the stress caused solely within the workplace (Earnshaw and Cooper, 1996). However, as our teachers have shown, the dynamic relationships between working and home lives make it difficult to separate out the sources and causes of stress, especially where spillover effects occur over some time. The teachers felt the school's part in precipitating their stress was not recognised by management, even though much has been written on the causes of teacher stress. They perceived their schools as interpreting stress in monolithic terms, generally identifying home factors or personal deficiencies as the cause, and therefore implicit in solutions. Moreover, individualised stress discourses and the scarce resources of time, personnel and finances available influenced management to take the view that support provision was not necessarily within the remit of the school. Luke's Head, for example, was 'very much into finance, won't support people out of the school budget plan' and asserted that 'some people who need to be supported shouldn't be supported by school processes but by other processes'. Yet, as we have shown, school processes were implicit in creating stress. Since organisations play their part in contributing to the downward spiral of the stress process, they must also take some responsibility for self-renewal processes (Fassel, 1992). Schools therefore need to develop and carry through formal policies regarding the recuperation of staff who suffer stress. The teachers felt the emotional welfare of members of staff was not only a legal issue but also a practical and moral one. 'It's obvious a school environment can help them get better' (Luke). As Jonathon declared,

> If you've paid lots of money to train someone, and you employ that person, you've a duty of care to make sure that person actually survives and does the job, and if they're failing in any area, a duty of care to identify that failure, and try and support them.

Teachers who are under stress need time and space to make the transition to the upward spiral. Some require an extended period away from the school environment to regain their health. During this time, they may need considerable advice and support to prevent too early a return to school. Some of our teachers used prescribed medication to facilitate returning to school when it was obvious that they were not yet fit to do so – sometimes due to pressures from management. The effects of sedation impaired their cognition and altered their behaviour, undermining their teaching competence and placing them at risk of further deterioration in health. School processes must be developed that encourage teachers not to compromise their health by returning to school too soon.

The Healthy Schools Initiative (www.wiredforhealth.gov.uk) and Teacherline (TBF, 2001) advocate the prompt provision of counselling. As we have seen, crisis counselling is all too often the norm. Peter Pyranty, manager-counsellor of the charity Stress at Work, described teachers he sees as 'wrecked. Physically and emotionally in a severe state ... I don't think I could make that generalization about any other profession. By the time teachers come to Stress at Work, a significant proportion are very severely damaged' (personal communication). Our findings show that counselling must not only be offered early on, as part of preventive, management and rehabilitative strategies, but that it must also match the needs of the individual teacher. Workplace counselling has many faces and the outcomes are highly dependent on the type and focus of the counselling provided. Many EAP programmes have been criticised for their emphasis on the individual adapting to the organisation (Newton *et al*, 1995). Effective workplace counselling also requires the scrutiny of the collective context (Carroll, 1996).

In addition, more care needs to be taken over who provides counselling. In the schools of most of our teachers, a member of the senior management team was responsible for dealing with troubled staff. This meant that the stressed teacher often received only informal counselling by someone who had little directed time and no great expertise. Yvonne was the stress facilitator in Walton Green, so was formally responsible for counselling troubled staff and students. Requiring a member of teaching or management staff to assume the role of workplace counsellor creates ethical dilemmas. Placed at the interface between the stressed individual and the school, while they are at the same time a member of its staff, they hold two sets of responsibilities which can often be irreconcilable. They need to show loyalty to the individual teacher or student and loyalty also to the school management and governors, and they may already have formed opinions about the emotionality of the teacher or student they are supposed to be helping. As Luke argued 'You can't be a reaching hand and an axe at the same time'.

There are, moreover, numerous ethical issues surrounding workplace counselling. There are problems in stepping outside the management role and into the counsellor role. When should confidentiality be broken, for example, in disclosing information about the stressed individual who may present a risk to the school or to pupils? Certain counselling approaches may have aims and values which are incompatible with school philosophies and policies. Which approaches should teacher counsellors choose to follow? When should teacher counsellors see stress as individual or as organisational and how should they decide whether and in what ways to bring organisational issues to the public domain, to 'help the organisation review and change workplace practices and policies that are antagonistic to human welfare' (Carroll, 1996:162)?

Counselling teachers is therefore a huge responsibility which requires well developed emotional literacy and ethical sensitivity. The work involves building bridges and mediation, necessitating 'the ability to see and interpret behaviour and its effects on others', and 'a realization that virtually any action may have ethical implications' (Carroll, 1996: 155). To develop these skills requires a good deal of training, and the work cannot just be tacked onto someone's job agenda. Teachers responsible for the emotional well-being of others are open to risk to their own health. Yvonne was one of a long line of individuals holding her post who succumbed to stress-related illnesses, demonstrating that the post itself was problematic. Indeed, according to Alex, soon after taking early retirement due to ill-health, Yvonne 'died for the cause'. Teacher counsellors themselves require protection from formal systems designed to explore and process workplace emotional issues, and space where they can safely discuss situations, knowledge, the possible consequences of specific decisions and outcomes, ethics and case reviews. In many service occupations, such as housing and social work, forms of work/clinical supervision (Holloway, 1995) are part of formal working conditions, with staff trained in peer supervision. In such situations, emotion within the workplace can be discussed and worked through in safety. Schools need to provide directed time, flexibility and safety for all teachers to access professional support such as Teacherline and Stress at Work in confidence and to make this provision part of policy.

The second issue in rehabilitation is to give teachers help to explore possible future options, so they can decide whether it is advisable to return to the teaching environment or whether to seek alternative opportunities. Those returning to their school might need to make a graduated return to the classroom. One of the main structural processes identified as hindering self-renewal was the requirement to return to work full time. Some local authorities and schools refused a gradual return that allowed the teacher to begin on a part-time basis. 'They said you're either fit to work or you're not fit to work. If you're fit to work you do full time. If you're not fit to work, you don't work, completely inflexible' (Luke). Luke suggested supporting re-entry with the aid of the supply teacher providing cover, as both salaries would need to be paid while the stressed teacher was considered unfit for full-time work.

School policy must include measures to deal ethically with teachers who are deemed 'unfit to teach' after suffering stress-related illness. While some of our teachers thought that their schools placed greater emphasis on protecting its reputation than on protecting its teachers, other schools in this sample sought both to protect themselves from accusations of diminishing student achievement, and to protect teachers from further harm. Some of our teachers refused to leave voluntarily when asked to do so, if they were not given support in gaining other employment. The experiences of William, Emily and Stephen suggest that certain schools invoke threats of competency proceedings, claiming that this was in the interests of safeguarding individual teacher health as well as school safety, student attainment and the school's reputation. William, for example, insisted on maintaining his teaching commitment despite all his problems and threatening competency proceedings was probably the only way to stop him returning to school. As Earnshaw and Cooper (1996: 113) write, 'at the end of the day, employers cannot be expected to employ indefinitely individuals who are incapable of carrying out their jobs. ... It may be more prudent to opt for dismissal rather than let him or her run the risk of stress-related illness.'

Our findings suggest furthermore, that certain teachers may be unable or unwilling to adapt to new ways of working or to a new corporate culture. For those who do not fit new cultures, formal ways of easing them into new employment areas without abusing them can be more humane than creating threats to their health. Some teachers in this sample felt that their skills as teachers were not transferable and for them, downshifting or relocating might be a suitable solution. However, several in our sample found rewarding new careers. If teaching is no longer a 'job for life', it would be appropriate for schools and external agencies dealing with 'outplacement' to provide career advice, creating portfolios and arranging interviews and training.

Schools must provide an ethically responsible working environment. Breaking the burnout cycle is in many ways, a resource issue. Most schools do not have the resources of money and time to implement organisational approaches to stress. This brings us back to the system level: these fundamental changes demand policy changes in the educational system at both local government and national level.

Individual level

There is much that individual teachers can do to tackle the stress within themselves and in their school. The first step is to acknowledge that we are all emotional beings. Men in particular may find that the emotional self is difficult to listen to and may fail to act on early signs. Feelings of loss of control are magnified by painful emotion, and they may find the stress experience emasculating. Both Andrew and Marcus declared that stress was 'for wimps'. Moynihan (1998: 13) observes that a man may recoil during illness 'in stoical silence, desperately eager to keep hold of the masculine identity that he's been taught is symbolic of strength and success as a man'. Illness thus disempowers. By the time some of our teachers sought help they were already experiencing a profound level of psychological and physical pain.

Helping yourself

* Seek help, and a space where you feel safe to declare your emotional state, your fears, and the extent of any illness.

* Find someone to trust – be it your GP, your spouse or a friend. Teachers may find it helpful to seek alliances with others. Some of Troman and Woods' (2001) sample of primary teachers, and Terence in our sample, joined a discussion group of senior teachers.

- Peer group discussion can offer the opportunity to dissipate stress, whereas problems may grow without it (Robertson, 1993).
- Seek out an independent agency such as Stress at Work. If you can't talk openly about your feelings, search the Internet for organisations such as Teacherline. There is plenty of help there if you are willing to seek and accept it.

Society expects its citizens to be academically literate. Much is made of the necessity to gain reading, writing, numeracy and technological skills, all of which are presented as empowering tools for opening the doors to employment and affluence. Although emotions are central to both private and public experience, they are low on the political agenda. Indeed, according to Goleman (1995: xi), the Western world is in the throes of a 'collective emotional crisis', where low levels of individual and organisational emotional literacy threaten prosperity. We have argued that low levels of emotional literacy contribute to the stress process.

While emotional literacy may be best developed in childhood (Steiner, 2000), life-long learning can also enhance individual competences. Traditional masculine socialisation may damage some men by rendering them 'less capable of having empathic, caring, intimate relationships with other people' (Kilmartin, 1994: 13). However, as the experiences of Alex, Luke and Maureen demonstrate, teachers can reduce some of the factors producing stress emotions by increasing their emotional literacy. We are all 'works in progress'. Emotional literacy training can help individuals under stressful conditions re-establish contact with their emotions. This is best done within a safe social relationship, finding at least one other person to learn with. The literature on emotional literacy is proliferating rapidly; there are vast resources on the internet, plus several organisations in Britain promoting emotional literacy training in schools, such as Antidote, Re-membering Education, and The Circle Works. Individual counselling training can prove helpful, as Alex found.

Developing higher levels of emotional skills and resilience

- Learn to recognise, differentiate and name your own feelings such as anger, fear, sadness, shame, guilt, pride and love. Learn what triggers these feelings, which are strongest and how to talk about them. Knowing your own feelings is the first step to judging how they affect you and those around you. Cultivating reflexivity and making space for it is important. Keeping a personal diary to record your reactions to events and monitor your feelings is a good way of externalising your feelings and making them available for analysis.
- Develop an empathic understanding of the emotions of others. Learn to read their feelings, identify with their motives and understand the reasons behind the strength of these feelings and their accompanying actions.
- Learn to manage your own emotions in ways that 'facilitate thought and action', and 'promote emotional and intellectual growth' (Salovey and Sluyter, 1997: 10). This involves understanding where and when to express emotion, whether positive or negative, in productive ways, and how emotional expression or its absence affects others.
- Recognise that we have to address the emotional harm we may cause. We all make mistakes. Not acknowledging mistakes damages relationships. We need to learn how to apologise for our mistakes and repair the hurt we cause. We do not always realise the effect we are having. Jeffrey and Woods (1998: 126) report a deputy head telling them how she asked a colleague whom she liked and worked with well to do something during preparations for a school inspection and saw: 'tears came to her eyes, and I thought 'Oh God, I've done it again!'...the end result of me trying to be helpful and efficient...was to make somebody fell really, really upset'.
- People at management or senior level are more likely to have an inflated view of their own emotional competence (Sala, 2001). Carroll (1996: 155) observes that 'many people do not see the implications of their behaviour on others'. Learning how others perceive you can significantly increase your own performance and that of others in your team.

One key facet of high levels of emotional literacy, as Margot and Luke both found, is knowing how to refuse tasks you do not wish to undertake, and which make you feel victimised. Our teachers found it difficult not to take on extra duties at schools with negative emotional climates where listening skills were poor, confidentiality compromised, and job security threatened. There is strength in alliances and numbers. Teachers need to develop collective coping skills in, for example, learning how to say 'no' when asked, or indeed told, to accept extra responsibilities that damage well-being. They need time to assess how workloads could be managed, what extra loads would cost in time and people's health, exploring how it feels to say 'no', and practising such responses within trusted social relationships. As Alex and Luke found, taking the journey towards becoming an 'emotional gourmet' improves transactions in all spheres of life. Developing what Steiner (2000) calls 'emotional interactivity' enables individuals to use a variety of emotional skills, ranging from simply recognising that they are themselves upset to calming down an upset student or colleague, to sensing the emotional interdependencies around them, seeing how, why and when emotions might escalate for better or worse, and how to use emotions productively, safely and ethically without harming others. Teachers can learn to increase their personal and social emotional competences such as self-awareness, empathy and communication. They can listen to others, and care for colleagues rather than censure those who are not coping.

You can begin to increase the level of emotional literacy within your school by working with your colleagues. Find at least one person who is interested in achieving a more emotionally literate workplace. Alex, for example, concentrated his efforts on a small group of teachers new to the department whom he considered more receptive to these ideas.

All teachers have an ethical responsibility to care for themselves, to nurture and maintain their physical, emotional, intellectual and spiritual well-being. They should ask themselves: How am I dealing with stress? How much alcohol do I drink? When do I reach for comfort food or a cigarette? How am I sleeping? Am I constantly tired? Do I wake early and worry? Do I have regular exercise? Do I recognise when I am angry, fearful, sad? When do I experience joy?

Several of our teachers found broadening their social network helpful. Alex, for example, reconnected with lost relatives and relocated to be nearer old friends. Hawkins and Shohet (1989: 17) suggest a method for mapping support systems that could be helpful for teachers. On a large piece of paper, draw yourself in the centre and surround yourself with symbols representing family members, friends, colleagues, professionals, social activities etc that comprise your present life support system. Include people from your past, for example parents and old friends that you still feel tied to. Are the ties between yourself and these people and activities strong or weak, close or distant? Draw how you use these ties. Analyse what attracts you to or blocks you from using particular pathways. Which energise you and which drains your energy? What is missing? Draw the links you would like to use but do not have. Explore with another person how you might nurture certain pathways, expand your resources and change your support system to serve you better.

The squeezing of time as stress radically reduces the positive things in life is an early danger sign. Jessica's spouse Kevin told us: 'When Jessica was getting knocked at school, it was affecting her whole outlook on life ... 100% of her time waking, apart from sleeping, was spent on school.' Create opportunities for gaining positive emotional experiences. Make time to be by yourself or with others, and seek a space for pleasure every day, whether this is taking exercise, making love, reading to yourself or a child, watching your favourite TV show or a movie, playing a musical instrument, meditating, or doing DIY. According to Goleman (1998), the daily practice of relaxation reduces the susceptibility to emotional distress by resetting neural pathways. Ensure you have even a small daily space where your thoughts and feelings are not focused on work. If work does not provide 'flow' (Czikszentmihalyi, 1990) in which you become positively engrossed in your undertaking, seek an alternative means outside your working life. Find a way to reclaim some childhood dream. Ann McGee-Cooper (1997: 178) experiences 'miraculous rejuvenation' after a busy day by tap dancing, which she took up in her late forties. Margot has her belly dancing, Luke and Alex their music. However, if this time and space is at the expense of others' emotional health, your relationships will continue to suffer.

Since teaching is widely acknowledged as a stressful occupation, teachers need to know about stress: its social aspects, its processual nature, and the connections between stress and illness. Teachers can take preventive measures by being more aware of the sources of stress, the multitude of symptoms, the range of coping strategies and whether these are constructive or counterproductive, and knowing where to access help. Those of our teachers who saw stress as an individual phenomenon tended to find the recovery process more problematic, while those who found it easier to recover tended to adopt a more organisationally based discourse regarding stress, often derived from the experience of union activities or other employment arenas. Increased knowledge will reduce feelings of self-blame and give some protection from loss of self. It helps to learn about the merits and disadvantages of various stress discourses. However, as the experiences of our teachers show, when stress is already threatening health and wellbeing, information of this type may do no more than help the stressed teacher to stay longer in post before 'hitting the wall', altering nothing in the long term unless school policies are changed.

Many stress reduction interventions require the individual to accommodate to the stress-inducing environment. This is seldom a successful long-term strategy. As Handy (1990: 26) argues '... the individually-oriented analyses and intervention strategies proposed by many stress or burnout researchers may simply divert attention away from organisational issues and help perpetuate the very problems they are designed to solve'. Individual teacher-based solutions tend to depoliticise stress. Accordingly they take no account of the effects of collective working experiences and practices, where shared perceptions, thoughts, feelings and actions produce collective adaptational processes, so affecting organisational health.

Although there are cases of individuals developing effective coping strategies, more successful solutions are achieved by modifying the culture, structure and functioning of the organisation. This brings us back to the wider context. A discourse of individual responsibility encourages individual pathologisation. In the words of Veninga and Spradley (1981: 6): 'like a thief in the night, work stress robs millions of workers of their health and happiness, then goes scot-free while the blame lies elsewhere'. Interventions at the level of school and educational system are therefore needed to prevent and deal satisfactorily with the experience of stress. As Clayton, cited in Comerford and Mansell, 1999, puts it: 'It is not the fault of the individual. It is the fault of the system'.

References

Abrams, J. and Zweig, C. (eds) (1991) *Meeting the Shadow: The Hidden Power of the Dark Side of Human Nature*, New York: Putman.

Acker, S. (1994) *Gendered Education: Sociological Reflections on Women, Teaching and Feminism*, Buckingham: Open University Press.

Advisory, Conciliation and Arbitration Services (ACAS) (1977) *Disciplinary Practice and Procedures in Employment*, London: ACAS.

Ankrah, E. M. (1991) 'AIDS and the social side of health', *Social Science and Medicine*, 32: 967-980.

Apple, M. W. (1986) *Teachers and Texts: A Political Economy of Class and Gender Relations in Education*, New York: Routledge and Kegan Paul.

Atkinson, R. (1998) *The Life Story Interview*, California: Sage.

Averill, J. (1996) 'An analysis of psychophysiological symbolism and its influence on theories of emotion', in Harré, R. and Parrott W. G. (eds) *The Emotions: Social, Cultural and Biological Dimensions*, London: Sage.

Ball, D. (1972) 'Self and identity in the context of deviance: The case of criminal abortion', in Scott, R. A. and Douglas, J. D. (eds) *Theoretical Perspectives on Deviance*, New York: Basic Books.

Ball, S. J. (1987) *The Micro-politics of the School: Towards a Theory of School Organisation*, London: Methuen.

Ball, S. J. (1990) *Politics and Policy-Making in Education*. London: Routledge.

Ball, S. J. (1998) 'Performativity and fragmentation in 'Postmodern Schooling", in J. Carter (ed.) *Postmodernity and Fragmentation of Welfare*. London: Routledge.

Ball, S. J. and Bowe, R. (1992) 'Subject departments and the 'implementation' of National Curriculum policy: an overview of the issues', *Journal of Curriculum Studies*, 24(2): 97-115.

Bartlett, D. (1998) *Stress: Perspectives and Processes*, Buckingham: Open University Press.

Beatty, B. R. (1999) 'Teachers and their leaders: the emotionality of teachers' relationships with administrators', paper presented at the International Study Association on Teachers and Teaching Conference, Dublin, June.

Berger, P. L. (1971) *A Rumour of Angels*, Harmondsworth: Penguin Books.

Berger, P. L., Berger, B. and Kellner, H. (1973) *The Homeless Mind*, Harmondsworth: Penguin Books.

Bergquist, W. H., Greenberg, E. M. and Klaum, G. A. (1993) *In Our Fifties: Voices of Men and Women Reinventing Their Lives*, San Francisco: Jossey-Bass.

Blackmore, J. (1996) 'Doing 'emotional labour' in the education market place: stories from the field of women in management', *Discourse: Studies in the Cultural Politics of Education*, 17(3): 337-349.

Blase, J. (1991) 'The micropolitical perspective', in Blase J. (ed) *The Politics of Life in Schools*, California: Sage.

Blase, J. and Anderson, G. (1995) *The Micropolitics of Educational Leadership: From Control to Empowerment,* London: Cassel.

Bolger, N., Delongis, A., Kessler, R. and Wethington, E. (1989) 'The contagion of stress across multiple roles', *Journal of Marriage and the Family*, 51: 175-183.

Boyle, G. J., Borg, M. G., Falzon, J. M. and Baglioni, A. J. (1995) 'A structural model of the dimensions of teacher stress', *British Journal of Educational Psychology,* 65: 49-67.

Brannen, J. M. (1988) 'Research note: the study of sensitive subjects: notes on interviewing', *The Sociological Review*, 36(3): 552-563.

Broadfoot, P. (1998) 'Quality standards and control in higher education: what price life-long learning?' *International Studies in Sociology of Education*, 8 (2): 155-181.

Brown, G. W. and Harris, T. O. (eds) (1989) *Life Events and Illness*, London: Hymen Urwin.

Brown, M. and Ralph, S. (1998) 'Change-linked work-related stress in teachers in England', paper presented at the British Educational Research Association Conference, Queens University, Belfast, August.

Bulan, H. F., Erickson, R. J. and Wharton A. S. (1997) 'Doing for others on the job: the affective requirements of service work, gender, and emotional well-being', *Social Problems*, 44 (2): 235-256.

Bunting, C. (1999) 'Call for mental-health aid in school', *The Times Educational Supplement,* June 25: 12.

Buyssen, H. (1996) *Traumatic Experiences of Nurses: When Your Profession Becomes a Nightmare,* London: Jessica Kingsley.

Byrne, B. (1995) 'The nomological network of teacher burnout: a literature review and empirically validated model', paper presented at the Teacher Burnout Conference, J. Jacobs Foundation, Marbach, Germany, November.

Campbell, R. J. and Neill, S. R. St J. (1994) *Primary Teachers at Work*, London: Routledge.

Carlyle, D. (2000) 'Opening the can of worms: gender and emotion in sensitive research', in Walford, G. and Hudson, C. (eds) *Genders and Sexualities in Educational Ethnography*, Oxford: Jai Press.

Carroll, M. (1996) *Workplace Counselling: A Systematic Approach to Employee Care*, London: Sage.

Chan, D. W. and Hui, E. K. P. (1995) 'Burnout and coping among Chinese secondary school teachers in Hong Kong', *British Journal of Educational Psychology*, 65: 15-25.

Clark, H., Chandler, J. and Barry, J. (1996) 'Work Psychology, Women and Stress: Silence, Identity and the Boundaries of Conventional Wisdom', *Gender, Work and Organisation*, 3(2): 65-77.

Clarke, J. and Newman, J. (1992) 'Managing to survive: dilemmas of changing organisational forms in the public sector', paper presented at Social Policy Association Conference, University of Nottingham, July.

Coles, M. (1997) 'Keep your head in the cultural revolution', *The Sunday Times*, December 17, (7): 18.

Comerford, C. and Mansell, W. (1999) 'Unions say torrent of stress claims pending', *Times Educational Supplement,* October 8: 7.

Cooper, C. L. (2000) *Stress at Work*, October 6, (http://www.stress.channel4.com).

Cooper, C. L. and Davidson, M. (1987) 'Sources of stress at work and their relations to stressors in non-working environments', in Kalmo, R., El-Batawi, M. A. and Cooper, C. L. (eds) *Psychosocial Factors at Work and their Relation to Health*, Geneva: World Health Organisation.

Cooper, P. and McIntyre, D. (1996) *Effective Teaching and Learning: Teachers and Students' Perspectives,* Buckingham: Open University Press.

Cooperstock, R. (1976) 'Women and psychotropic drugs', in MacLennan, A. (ed) *Women: Their Use of Alcohol and Other Legal Drugs*, Toronto: Addiction Research Foundation.

Court, M. (1994) 'Removing macho management: lessons from the field of education', *Gender, Work and Organization*, 1(1): 33-49.

Cox, T., Boot N. and Cox S. (1989) 'Stress in schools: a problem-solving approach', in Cole, M. and Walker, S. (eds) *Teaching and Stress*, Milton Keynes: Open University Press.

Crawford, J., Kippax, S., Onyx, J., Gault, U. and Benton P. (1992) *Emotion and Gender: Constructing Meaning from Memory*, London: Sage.

Crawford, M. (1997) 'Managing stress in educational organisations', in Crawford, M., Kidd, L. and Riches, C. (eds) *Leadership and Teams in Educational Management,* Buckingham: Open University Press.

Czikszentmihalyi, M. (1990) *Flow: The Psychology of Optimal Experience*, New York: Harper and Collins

Denzin, N. (1984) *On Understanding Emotion*, San Francisco: Jossey-Bass.

Department for Education and Employment (DfEE) (1998) *Teachers: Meeting the Challenge of Change*, Green Paper Cm 4164, London: HMSO.

Department for Education and Employment (DfEE) (1999) 'Encourage creativity in schools says new report' *DfEE Paper 215/99*, London: DfEE, 14 May.

Department for Education and Skills (DfES) (2001) *Green Paper on Schools: Building on Success*, London: HMSO (http://www.dfes.gov.uk/buildingon success).

Department for Education and Skills (DfES) (2002a) *Statistics of Education: Teachers in England; 2001 Edition,* London: The Stationery Office.

Department for Education and Skills (DfES) (2002b) *Green Paper on extending opportunities and raising standards for 14 to 19 year olds*, London: DfES (http://www.dfes.gov.uk/14-19greenpaper).

Department for Education and Skills (DfES) (2002c) *Education and Skills: Delivering Results, a Strategy to 2006*, London, DfES (http://www.dfes.gov.uk/ delivering-results/contents.shtml).

Department of Health (DoH) (1999) Saving Lives: Our Healthier Nation, London: HMSO, (http://www.archive.official-documents.co.uk/document/cm43/4386/4386).

Dinham, S. (1993) 'Teachers under stress', *Australian Educational Researcher*, 20(3): 1-16.

Dinham, S. and Scott, C. (1996) *The Teacher 2000 Project: A Study of Teacher Satisfaction, Motivation and Health*, Sidney: University of Western Sydney, Nepean.

Doyle, J. A. (1989) *The Male Experience*, Iowa: Wm. C. Brown.

Draper, J. (1992) The Creation of Lymescroft School: An Ethnographic Study of Some Aspects of a School Merger, unpublished PhD thesis, Open University.

Dunham, J. (1992) *Stress in Teaching*, 2nd edition, London: Routledge.

Earnshaw, J. and Cooper C. L. (1996) *Stress and Employer Liability*, London: Institute of Personnel and Development.

Education Service Advisory Committee (1998) *Managing Work-Related Stress: A Guide for Mangers and Teachers in the Schools* (2nd edition), London: HMSO.

Eisler, R. M. and Blalock, J. A. (1991) 'Masculine gender role stress: implications for the assessment of men', *Clinical Psychology Review*, 11: 45-60.

Ekman, P. and Davidson R. J. (1994) *The Nature of Emotion: Fundamental Questions*, New York: Oxford University Press.

Elkind, D. (1994) *Ties that Stress: The New Family Imbalance,* Cambridge, Mass: Harvard University Press.

European Commission, Directorate-General for Employment and Social Affairs, (2000) *Guidance on work-related stress: Spice of life – or kiss of death*, (http://www.ilo.org).

Farber, B. A. (1991) *Crisis in Education: Stress and Burnout in the American Teacher*, San Francisco: Jossey-Bass.

Fassel, D. (1992) *Working Ourselves to Death: The High Costs of Workaholism and the Rewards of Recovery*, London: Thorsons.

Fielding, M. (2001) 'Taking education really seriously: four years' hard labour' in Fielding, M. (ed.) *Taking Education Really Seriously: Four Years' Hard Labour,* London: Routledge/Falmer.

Fineman, S. (ed) (1993) *Emotion in Organizations,* London: Sage.

Fitz, J. (1994) 'Implementation research and education policy: practice and prospects', *British Journal of Educational Studies*, 42 (1): 53-69.

Folkman, S. (1997) 'Positive psychological states and coping with severe stress', *Social Science and Medicine*, 45(8): 1207-1221.

Freudenberger, H. J. with Richelson G. (1980) *Burnout: The High Cost of High Achievement*, New York: Anchor Press.

Freund, P. E. S. (1990) 'The expressive body: a common ground for the sociology of emotions and health and illness', *Sociology of Health and Illness*, 12(4): 452-477.

Friedman, I. A. (1991) 'High- and low-burnout schools: school culture aspects of teacher burnout', *Journal of Educational Research*, 84(6): 325-333.

Fullan, M. (1997) 'Emotion and hope: constructive concepts for complex times', in Fullan, M. (ed) *The Challenge of School Change*, Arlington Heights: Skylight.

Garfinkel, H. (1956) 'Conditions of successful degradation ceremonies', *American Journal of Sociology*, 61: 420-4.

Gewirtz, S. and Ball, S. J. (2000) 'From 'Welfarism' to 'New Managerialism': shifting discourses of school headship in the education marketplace', *Discourse: Studies in the Cultural Politics of Education*, 21(3) 253-268.

Giddens, A. (1984) *The Constitution of Society: Outline of a Theory of Structuration*, Cambridge: Polity Press.

Giddens, A. (1990) *The Consequences of Modernity*, Cambridge: Polity Press.

Giddens, A. (1991) *Modernity and Self-Identity*, Cambridge: Polity Press.

Ginn, J. and Sandell, J. (1997) 'Balancing home and employment: stress reported by social services staff', *Work, Employment and Society*, 11(3): 413-434.

Glaser, B. G. and Strauss, A. L. (1971) *Status Passage,* Chicago: Aldine.

Goffman, E. (1959) *The Presentation of Self in Everyday Life*, New York: Doubleday.

Goffman, E. (1961) *Asylums,* Harmondsworth: Penguin Books.

Goffman, E. (1964) *Stigma, Notes on the Management of the Spoiled Identity*, New Jersey: Prentice Hall.

Goleman, D. (1995) *Emotional Intelligence*, New York: Bantam Books.

Goleman, D. (1998) *Working with Emotional Intelligence,* London: Bloomsbury.

Goleman, D. (2001) 'An EI-Based Theory of Performance', in Cherniss, C. and Goleman, D. (eds) *The Emotionally Intelligent Workplace, The Consortium for Research on Emotional Intelligence in Organizations*, (http://www.eiconsortuim.org).

Goleman, D., Cherniss, C. *et al*, (2001) *The Consortium for Research on Emotional Intelligence in Organizations*, (http://www.eiconsortuim.org).

Gomer, H. (1999) 'People firms are happier firms', *The Sunday Telegraph*, Business File, September 19: 1.

Gottman, J. M., Katz L. F. and Hooven, C. (1997) *Meta-Emotion: How Families Communicate Emotionally*, New Jersey: Lawrence Erlbaum.

Griffith, J., Steptoe, A. and Cropley, M. (1999) 'An investigation of coping strategies associated with job stress in teachers', *British Journal of Educational Psychology*, 69(4): 517-532.

Halton, W. (1995) 'Institutional stress on providers in health and education', *Psychodynamic Counselling*, 1(2): 187-198.

Hammersley, M. and Atkinson, P. (1995) *Ethnography: Principles in Practice*, London: Routledge.

Handy, J. (1990) *Occupational Stress in a Caring Profession*, Aldershot: Avebury.

Handy, J. (1995) 'Rethinking stress: seeing the collective', in Newton, T. with Handy, J. and Fineman, S. (1995) *'Managing' Stress: Emotion and Power at Work*, London: Sage.

Hansen, E. H. (1989) 'How widely do women and men differ in their use of psychotropic drugs?' *Journal of Social and Administrative Pharmacy*, 6(4): 165-183.

Hargreaves, A. (1994) *Changing Teachers, Changing Times*, London: Cassell.

Hargreaves, A. (1998a) 'The emotional practice of teaching', *Teaching and Teacher Education*, 14(8): 835-854.

Hargreaves, A. (1998b) 'The emotional politics of teaching and teacher development: with implications for educational leadership', *International Journal of Leadership in Education,* 1(4): 315-336.

Hargreaves, A. (1999) 'Teaching in a box: emotional geographies of teaching', keynote address presented to the International Study Association on Teachers and Teaching Conference, Dublin, June.

Hargreaves, A. and Fullan, M. (1998) *What's Worth Fighting For in Education*, Buckingham: Open University Press.

Hargreaves, A. and Tucker, E. (1991) 'Teaching and guilt: exploring the feelings of teaching', *Teaching and Teacher Education*, 7(5/6): 491-505.

Hawkins, P. and Shohet, R. (1989) *Supervision in the Helping Professions: an individual, group and organizational approach*, Milton Keynes: Open University Press.

Health and Safety Executive (HSE) (1990) *Managing Occupational Stress: A Guide for Managers and Teachers in the School Sector*, Sheffield: Health and Safety Commission.

Health and Safety Executive (HSE) (1995) *Stress at Work: A Guide for Employers,* Suffolk: HSE Books.

Health Education Authority (1988) *Stress in the Public Sector: Nurses, Police, Social Workers and Teachers*, London: Health Authority.

Helsby, G. (1999) *Changing Teachers' Work: The Reform of Secondary Schooling*, Buckingham: Open University Press.

Henry, J. (2000) '£250,000 – the price of a ruined career', *Times Educational Supplement,* December 8: 7.

Henry, T. (1994) 'From Jurassic Park to Meatloaf', paper presented at the Medical Advice and Advisory Group Conference, York, March.

Hochschild, A. R. (1979) 'Emotion work, feeling rules, and social structure', *American Journal of Sociology*, 85(3): 551-575.

Hochschild, A. R. (1983) *The Managed Heart*, California: Berkeley University Press.

Hochschild, A. R. (1997) *The Time Bind: When Work becomes Home and Home becomes Work*, New York: Metropolitan Books.

Holloway, E. L. (1995) *Clinical Supervision: A System Approach*, California: Sage.

Hopkins, V. (1997) 'Optimising performance for your organisation: strategic interventions', presentation at the Healthier Organisations Seminar, Stress At Work, Northampton, November 12.

Hudson, F. M. (1991) *The Adult Years: Mastering the Art of Self-renewal,* San Francisco: Jossey-Bass.

Hyden, L-C. (1997) 'Illness and narrative', *Sociology of Health and Illness:* 48-69.

James, N. (1989) 'Emotional labour: skill and work in the social regulation of feelings', *The Sociological Review*: 15-42.

Jeffrey, B. and Woods P. (1996) 'Feeling de-professionalized: the social construction of teacher emotions during an OFSTED inspection', *Cambridge Journal of Education* 26, (3): 325-343.

Jeffrey, B. and Woods, P. (1998) *Testing Teachers: The Effect of School Inspections on Primary Teachers*, London: Falmer Press.

Kaluzny, A. D., McLaughlin, C. P. and Simpson, K. (1992) 'Applying total quality management concepts to public health organisations', *Public Health Reports – Hyattsville*, 107(3): 257-264.

Kanter, R. M. (1992) *When Giants Learn to Dance: Mastering the Challenges of Strategy, Management, and Careers in the 1990s,* London: Routledge.

Kelchtermans, G. (1995) 'Teacher stress and burnout', summary of the Teacher Burnout Conference, J. Jacobs Foundation, Marbach, Germany, November.

Kelchtermans, G. (1996) 'Teacher vulnerability: understanding its moral and political roots', *Cambridge Journal of Education*, 26(3): 307- 323.

Kemper, T. D. (1978) *A Social Interactional Theory of Emotions,* New York: Wiley and Sons.

Kilmartin, C. T. (1994) *The Masculine Self*, New York: Macmillan.

Kitchens, J. A. (1994) *Talking to Ducks: Rediscovering the Joy and Meaning in your Life,* New York: Fireside.

Klein, R. (1997) 'Emotional appeal', *The Times Educational Supplement*, 2, September 26: 4-5.

Kubler-Ross, E. (1975) *Death: The Final Stage of Growth*, New Jersey: Prentice-Hall.

Kyriacou, C. (1987) 'Teacher stress and burnout: an international review', *Educational Research*, 29(2): 146-152.

Kyriacou, C. (2000) *Stress-Busting for Teachers*, Cheltenham: Stanley Thornes (Publishers) Ltd.

Kyriacou, C. and Harriman, P. (1993) 'Teacher stress and the school merger', *School Organisation*, 13: 297-302.

Lankard, B. A. (1993) *Career Development through Self-Renewal*, ERIC Clearinghouse on Adult, Career, and Vocational Education, Columbus, Ohio.

Lazarus, R. S. (1990) 'Stress, coping and illness', in Friedman, H. S. (ed) *Personality and Disease*, New York: John Wiley.

Lazarus, R. S. and Lazarus, B. N. (1994) *Passion and Reason: Making Sense of Our Emotions*, New York: Oxford University Press.

Lee, R. (1993) *Doing Research on Sensitive Topics*, London: Sage.

Leithwood, K., Menzies, T., Jantzi, D. and Leithwood, J. (1995) 'Teacher burnout: a critical challenge for leaders of restructuring schools', paper presented at the Teacher Burnout Conference, J. Jacobs Foundation, Marbach, Germany, November.

Leventhal, H. and Patrick-Miller, L. (1993) 'Emotion and illness: the mind is in the body', in Lewis, M. and Haviland, J. M. (eds) *Handbook of Emotions*, New York: Guildford Press.

Lewis, S. and Cooper, C. (1983) 'The stress of combining occupational and parental roles: a review of the literature', *Bulletin of the British Psychological Society*, 36: 341-345.

Little, J. W. (1990) 'The persistence of privacy: autonomy and initiative in teachers' professional relations', *Teachers' College Record*, 91(4): 509-36.

Litwin, G. H., Humphrey, J. W. and Wilson, T. B. (1978) 'Organizational climate: a proven tool for improving performance', in Burke, W. (ed) *The Cutting Edge: Current Theory and Practice in Organization Development,* California: University Associates.

Margolis, D. R. (1998) *The Fabric of Self: A Theory of Ethics and Emotions*, New Haven: Yale University Press.

Marris, P. (1993) *Loss and Change*, London: Routledge.

McGee-Cooper, A. (1997) 'You don't have to come home from work exhausted' in Allenbaugh, K. (1997) (ed) *Chocolate for a Woman's Soul: 77 Stories to Feed Your Spirit and Warm Your Heart*, New York: Simon and Schuster.

McHugh, M. and Kyle, M. (1993) 'School merger: a stressful challenge?', *School Organisation*, 13: 11-26.

McLaren, P. (1986) *Schooling as a Ritual Performance,* London, Routledge and Kegan Paul.

Mearns, D. and Thorne, B. (1988) *Person-centred Counselling in Action*, London: Sage.

Menter, I., Muschamp, Y., Nicholls, P., Ozga, J. with Pollard, A. (1997) *Work and Identity in the Primary School*, Buckingham, Open University Press.

Mills, S. H. (1990) *Stress Management for Teachers,* Lancaster: Framework Press.

Mills, S. H. (1995) *Stress Management for the Individual Teacher*, Lancaster: Framework Press.

Milne, S. (1998) 'Managers under stress: 'new workplace bullies'', *The Guardian*, December 1: 7.

Morgan, D. H. J. (1996) *Family Connections: An Introduction to Family Studies*, Cambridge: Polity Press.

Morokoff, P. J. and Gilliland, R. (1993) 'Stress, sexual functioning, and marital satisfaction', *The Journal of Stress Research*, 30(1): 43-53.

Morris, E. (2001) 'Professionalism and Trust – the future of teachers and teaching', A speech by the Rt Hon Estelle Morris MP Secretary of State of Education and Skills to the Social Market Foundation, London: Department for Education and Skills (DfES).

Moynihan, C. (1998) 'Strength in silence', *The Guardian*, October 20(2): 13.

Musgrove, F. M. (1977) *Margins of the Mind,* London: Methuen.

National Advisory Committee on Creative and Cultural Education (NACCCE) (1999) *All Our Futures: Creativity, Culture and Education*, London, DfEE.

National Association of Schoolmasters Union of Women Teachers (NASUWT) (1996) *No Place to Hide: Confronting Workplace Bullies*, Birmingham: NASUWT.

National Union of Teachers (NUT) (1990) *Health and Safety: Teachers, Stress and Schools,* London: National Union of Teachers.

National Work-stress Network News (2001), Winter: 3, brian.robinson@nasuwt.net.

Neustatter, A. (2000) 'Hard day at the office, dear?' *The Guardian*, January 11: 6.

Newton, T. with Handy, J. and Fineman, S. (1995) *'Managing' Stress: Emotion and Power at Work*, London: Sage.

Nias, J. (1989) *Primary Teachers Talking: A Study of Teaching as Work*, London: Routledge.

Nias, J. (1991) 'Changing times, changing identities; grieving for a lost self', in R.G. Burgess, (ed.) *Educational Research and Evaluation*, London, Falmer Press.

Nias, J. (1996) 'Thinking about feeling: the emotions in teaching', *Cambridge Journal of Education*, 26(3): 293-306.

Oakley, A. (1974) *Housewife*, London: Allen Lane.

Oatley, K. (1996) 'Emotions: communications to the self and others', in Harré, R. and Parrott, W. G. (eds) *The Emotions: Social, Cultural and Biological Dimensions*, London: Sage.

Obholzer, A. and Roberts, V. Z. (1994) *The Unconscious at Work: Individual and Organizational Stress in the Human Services*, London: Routledge.

O'Reilly, J. (1999) 'Inspectors identify 15,000 bad teachers', *The Sunday Times*, January 31: 3.

Osborn, M, (1995) 'Not a seamless robe: a tale of two teachers' responses to policy change', paper presented at the European Conference on Educational Research, Bath University, September.

Parkinson, B. (1995) *Ideas and Realities of Emotion,* London: Routledge.

Parkinson, B. (1996) 'Emotions are social', *British Journal of Psychology*, 87: 663-683.

Passmore, B. (1997) 'Stressed-out heads reach for Prozac', *Times Educational Supplement*, November 7: 9.

Paterson, A. S. (1997) 'A humanistic framework for interviewer skills', paper presented at Student British Educational Research Association, York, August.

Phillips, T. (1999) 'Knowing me, knowing you', *Times Educational Supplement*, December 10: 19.

Pines, A. M. and Aronson, E. with Kafry, D. (1981) *Burnout: From Tedium to Personal Growth*, New York: Free Press.

Pithers, R. T. (1995) 'Teacher stress research: problems and progress', *British Journal of Educational Psychology*, 65: 387-392.

PricewaterhouseCoopers (2001) *Teacher Workload Study: Final Report*, London: PwC.

Punch, K. F. and Tuettemann, E. (1991) 'Stressful factors and the likelihood of psychological distress among classroom teachers', *Educational Research*, 33(1): 65-69.

Radley, A. (1994) *Making Sense of Illness: The Social Psychology of Health and Disease*, London: Sage.

Rafferty, F. (1997) 'Pension rule battle goes to court', *Times Educational Supplement*, January 10: 3.

Redwood, F. (1998) 'Stress in the classroom is a family affair', *The Sunday Times*, March 1, 7: 23.

Revell, P. (2000) 'The cost of workplace overload', *Times Educational Supplement,* May 26: 31.

Rice, R. W. (1984) 'Organizational work and the overall quality of life', in Oskamp, S. (ed) *Applied Social Psychology Annual 5*, Beverly Hills, California: Sage.

Richardson, G. (1995) 'Leaving the profession', in Bell, J. (ed) *Teachers Talk about Teaching: Coping with Change in Turbulent Times*, Buckingham: Open University Press.

Riseborough, G. F. (1981) 'Teacher Careers and Comprehensive Schooling: an empirical study', *Sociology,* 15(3): 352-81.

Robbins, A. (1992) *Awaken the Giant Within: How to take immediate control of your mental, emotional, physical and financial destiny*, New York: Simon and Schuster.

Robertson, N. (1993) 'Tackling stress in the workplace', *Audit Trends,* 1(1): 9-10.

Robinson, D. (1997) 'Why do some teachers 'rush for the door'?' *The Chronicle and Echo*, Northampton, January 30: 32-33.

Rogers, L. and Rayment, T. (1995) 'Stress explosion', *The Sunday Times,* December 31, 1: 12.

Rowbotham, S. (1973) *Woman's Consciousness, Man's World,* Harmondsworth: Penguin Books.

Rubin, H. J. and Rubin, I. S. (1995) *Qualitative Interviewing; The Art of Hearing Data,* California: Sage.

Rudow, B. (1995) 'Stress and burnout in the teaching profession: European studies, issues and research perspectives', paper presented at the Teacher Burnout Conference, J. Jacobs Foundation, Marbach, Germany, November.

Russo, N. F. (1976) 'The motherhood mandate', *Journal of Social Issues*, 32: 143-154.

Sala, F. (2001) Do Programmes Designed to Increase Emotional Literacy at Work Work? Consortium for Research on Emotional Intelligence in Organizations, (http://www.eiconsortuim.org).

Salmon, J. (1997) 'Ill-health blamed for exodus of staff', *The Times Educational Supplement*, September 17: 3.

Salovey, P. and Sluyter, D. J. (eds) (1997) *Emotional Development and Emotional Intelligence: Educational Implications*, New York: Basic Books.

Sarason, S. B. (1996) *Barometers of Change: Individual, Educational and Social Transformation*, San Francisco: Jossey-Bass.

Scheff, T. J. (1990) *Microsociology: Discourse, Emotion, and Social Structure,* Chicago: University of Chicago Press.

Seidman, S. A. and Zager, J. (1991) 'A study of coping behaviours and teacher burnout', *Work and Stress*, 5(3): 205-216.

Selye, H. (1974) *Stress without Distress*, New York: Harper and Row.

Shillaker, D. (1997) 'Stress at work: an underwriter's view', paper presented at the National Work-stress Network (NWN) First National Conference, Birmingham, March.

Shweder, R. A. (1994) 'You're not sick, you're just in love: emotion as an interpretive system', in Ekman, P. and Davidson, R. J. (eds) *The Nature of Emotion: Fundamental Questions*, New York: Oxford University Press.

Sieber, J. E. (1992) *Planning Ethically Responsible Research: A Guide for Students and Internal Review Boards*, Applied Social Science Research Methods Series, 31, California: Sage.

Smith, P. (1992) *The Emotional Labour of Nursing: How Nurses Care*, London: Macmillan.

Smithers, A. and Robinson, P. (1998) 'Can there ever be enough teachers?' *The Times Educational Supplement,* April 24: 20.

Snow, D. and Anderson, L. (1987) 'Identity work among the homeless: the verbal construction and avowal of personal identities', *American Journal of Sociology,* 92(6): 1336-1371.

Sparkes, A. C. (1990) 'Power, domination and resistance in the process of teacher-initiated innovation', *Research Papers in Education*, 5(2): 153-178.

Stapley, L. (1996) *The Personality of the Organisation: A Psychodynamic Explanation of Culture and Change,* London: Free Association Books.

Steiner, C. (2000) *Emotional Literacy: Intelligence with a Heart*, (http://www.emotional-literacy.com).

Stewart, I. and Joines, V. (1987) *TA Today: A New Introduction to Transactional Analysis*, Nottingham: Lifespace Publishing.

Strauss, A. L. (1987) *Qualitative Analysis for Social Scientists,* Cambridge: Cambridge University Press.

Strauss, A. L. and Corbin, J. (1990) *Basics of Qualitative Research: Grounded Theory Procedures and Techniques*, Newbury Park: Sage.

Strauss, A., Fagerhaugh, S., Suczek, B. and Wiener, C. (1985) *Social Organisation of Medical Work*, Chicago: University of Chicago Press.

Sutcliffe, J. (1997) 'Enter the feel-bad factor: a survey of teachers' attitudes reveals a tired, angry profession with an agenda for change', *Times Educational Supplement*, January 10: 1.

Taylor, A. and Hill, F. (1993) 'Quality management in education', *Quality Assurance in Education*, 1(1): 21-28.

Teachers Benevolent Fund (TBF) (2000) *Teacherline: First Report. Managing Stress in School*, London: TBF, May.

Teachers Benevolent Fund (TBF) (2001) *Teacherline: Progress Report*, London: TBF, September.

Tilden, V. P. and Gaylen, R. D. (1987) 'Cost and conflict: the darker side of social support', *Western Journal of Nursing Research*, 9(1): 9-18.

Travers, C. J. and Cooper, C. L. (1996) *Teachers Under Pressure*, London: Routledge.

Troman, G. (1996) 'Models of the 'good' teacher: defining and redefining teacher quality', in Woods, P. (ed) *Contemporary Issues in Teaching and Learning*, London: Routledge.

Troman, G. (1999) 'Experiencing naming, blaming and shaming: teacher stress in a 'failing' school', paper presented at the British Educational Research Association Conference, University of Sussex, September.

Troman, G. and Woods, P. (2001) *Primary Teachers' Stress*, London: RoutledgeFalmer.

Turner, B. S. (1987) *Medical Power and Social Knowledge*, London: Sage.

Turner, V. W. (1969) *The Ritual Process*, London: Routledge and Kegan Paul.

Turner, V. W. (1979) *Process, Performance and Pilgrimage*, New Delhi, Concept.

Van Eck, M., Nicolson, N. A. and Berkhof, J. (1998) 'Effects of stressful daily events on mood states: relationship to global perceived stress', *Journal of Personality and Social Psychology*, 75(6): 1572-1585.

Van Gennep, A. (1960) *The Rites of Passage*, London: Routledge and Kegan Paul.

Van Someren, L. (1998) 'New developments on the life events scale', *Stress News, Journal of the International Stress Management Association* (UK branch), 10(3): 7.

Veninga, R. L. and Spradley, J. P. (1981) *The Work-stress Connection: How to Cope with Job Burnout*, Boston: Little, Brown and Company.

Wallace, M. (1993) 'Discourse of derision: the role of the mass media within the education policy process', *Journal of Education Policy*, 8(4): 321-337.

Wallace, W. (1997) 'Double act: teachers as parents', *Times Educational Supplement,* (2), September 5: 3-4.

Weller, L. D. and Hartley, S. H. (1994) 'Total quality management and school restructuring: Georgia's approach to educational reform', *Quality Assurance in Education,* 2(2): 18-25.

Westman, M. and Etzion, D. (1995) 'Crossover of stress, strain and resources from one spouse to another', *Journal of Organizational Behavior,* 16: 169-181.

Westman, M. and Vinokur, A. D. (1998) 'Unravelling the relationship of distress levels within couples: common stressors, empathic reactions, or crossover via social interaction', *Human Relations*, 51(2): 137-156.

Wilkinson, R. G. (1996) *Unhealthy Societies: The Afflictions of Inequality*, London: Routledge.

Williams, S. J. (1998) 'Capitalising' on emotions? Rethinking the inequalities in health debate', *Sociology*, 32(1): 121-139.

Williams, S. J. (2000) 'Chronic illness as biographical disruption or biographical disruption as chronic illness? Reflections on a core concept', *Sociology of Health and Illness*, 22(1): 40-67.

Williams, S. J. and Bendelow, G. (1996) 'Emotions, health and illness: the 'missing link' in medical sociology', in James, V. and Gabe, J. (eds) *Health and the Sociology of Emotions*, Oxford: Blackwell.

Woods, P. (1992) 'Symbolic interactionism: theory and method', in LeCompte, M. D., Millroy, W. L. and Preissle, J. (eds) *The Handbook of Qualitative Research in Education*, London: Academic Press Inc.

Woods, P. (1993) *Critical Events in Teaching And Learning*, London: Falmer Press.

Woods, P. (1995) 'Intensification and stress in teaching', paper presented at the Teacher Burnout Conference, J. Jacobs Foundation, Marbach, Germany, November.

Woods, P. (1996a) 'Research proposal on 'Primary Teachers' Stress and Burnout', submitted to The Economic and Social Research Council, Milton Keynes: Open University.

Woods, P. (1996b) *Researching the Art of Teaching: Ethnography for Educational Use*, London: Routledge.

Woods, P. and Jeffrey, B. (1996) *Teachable Moments: The Art of Teaching in Primary Schools*, Buckingham: Open University Press.

Woods, P. and Jeffrey, B. (2002) 'The reconstruction of primary teachers' identities', *The British Journal of Sociology of Education*, 23(1): 89-106.

Woods, P. and Wenham, P. (1995) 'Politics and pedagogy: a case study in appropriation', *Journal of Education Policy*, 10(3): 119-141.

Woods, P., Jeffrey, B., Troman, G. and Boyle, M. (1997) *Restructuring Schools, Reconstructing Teachers: Responding to change in the primary school,* Buckingham: Open University Press.

Zaccaro, S. J., Blair V., Peterson C. and Zazanis, M. (1995) 'Collective Efficacy', in Maddux J. E. *Self-efficacy, Adaptation, and Adjustment: Theory, Research and Application*, New York: Plenum Press.

Subject Index

Author Index